The Popper
PENGUIN
RESCUE

ISBN 979-11-91343-24-3 14740

Longtail Books

The Popper
PENGUIN
RESCUE

Inspired by the Newbery Honor Book
Mr. Popper's Penguins
by Richard and Florence Atwater

BY ELIOT SCHREFER
ILLUSTRATED BY JIM MADSEN

To the memory of Florence and Richard Atwater and their children, Doris Atwater and Carroll Atwater Bishop.

Our grandparents' book, *Mr. Popper's Penguins,* has delighted children for decades. It has been translated into numerous languages and has inspired theatrical, musical, and film adaptations. Now it has inspired a new book, *The Popper Penguin Rescue.* We hope that you enjoy it.

—Kate and Alec Bishop

STILLWATER

EACH YEAR, STILLWATER held the Popper **parade**, when everyone would **gather** to **acknowledge** the city's most famous **resident**s. Grown-ups took the day off work. No children had to go to classes.

There was good reason to **celebrate** the Poppers. Mr. Popper had once been an **ordinary** house painter. But he'd fallen in love with penguins and let his favorite **explore**r know. Then, one September thirtieth, he'd received a penguin, sent express mail straight from the **Antarctic** by Admiral[1] Drake himself!

That now-famous penguin, Captain Cook[2], was soon followed by another, Greta. Once there were a male and female penguin in the house, there were eggs and **chicks**. The Poppers soon **host**ed twelve penguins and became very famous after they started up a traveling **theatrical** act.

From then on, September thirtieth was Stillwater's Popper parade day. The **local** children would take the bus to school as usual, but they'd **cluster** in the **schoolyard** instead of going to classes. There, they **don**ned their best penguin **costume**s, which they had worked hard on in art class. Some looked very **accurate**. Some looked more like skunks or hamsters.

The adults in the town arrived next, dressed like the Poppers or the other characters from the family's adventure—Mrs. Callahan, Mr. Greenbaum, even Admiral Drake himself! Everyone would have great fun wearing **elegant** clothes from the 1930s. Then, with the high school **marching** band **blaring** away, they all **proceed**ed around town. The kids went first, doing their best

---

1 Admiral 제독. 해군의 함대 사령관 또는 해군 장성에 대한 통칭.
2 Captain Cook 영국의 탐험가이자 항해가인 제임스 쿡(James Cook)에게서 따온 이름. 그의 탐험으로 현재와 거의 같은 태평양 지도가 만들어졌다.

impressions of a penguin **waddle**. The group **trundled** past the former Popper home at 432 Proudfoot Avenue, past the **barber** shop and the Palace Theater. The **procession** finished at the great city square, where news crews came from all over the country to film the **merriment**.

In the square were copper[3] **statue**s of all twelve Popper Penguins: Captain Cook, Greta, Columbus, Victoria, Nelson, Jenny, Magellan, Adelina, Scott, Isabella, Ferdinand, and Louisa. In the center of those birds were statues of the Poppers and their children. It made quite an image for the front pages of the nation's newspapers. Confetti[4] and ribbons, penguins and Poppers! It was the **highlight** of every year in Stillwater.

Across the river, in Hillport, it was quite a different story.

---

3 copper 구리 또는 동. 붉은색의 광택이 나는 금속으로 비교적 무르고 가공하기 쉬우며, 열과 전기의 전도율이 높아 실생활에 널리 쓰인다.

4 confetti 결혼식이나 축제 등의 특별한 행사에서 뿌리는 색종이 조각.

HILLPORT

AFTER PASSING THROUGH the **neat boulevard**s of Stillwater, the moving truck **rumble**d past the low houses and **blink**ing **billboard**s of Hillport. The town had every kind of penguin **attraction** imaginable. There were penguin **pet**ting zoos,[1] penguin gift shops, even

---

1 petting zoo 일반적인 동물원과 달리 사람들이 직접 동물을 만지며 체험할 수 있는 특별한 동물원을 말한다.

a penguin waterslide. The truck eventually came to a stop in front of a sagging building. Light bulbs traced the words *Penguin Pavilion* out front, but not a single bulb was lit, despite the dark evening. The front door of the broken-down petting zoo was boarded up, and the electricity was shut off.

"We're going to live *here*, Mom?" Joel asked, rubbing the car window with his sleeve so he could see better. He didn't mean his words to sound as negative as they did.

"Is there even any power?" asked his little sister, Nina, from the middle seat of the moving truck.

"I have a call in to the electric company," their mother said. "They'll have it back on as soon as they can. Come on, kids, I need you to be flexible and understanding for a few days."

"Are there really going to be *penguins* living inside?" Nina asked, climbing over Joel so she could press her face against the fogged side window. She wiped it with her hand, but her breath immediately fogged it right back up. Joel could see what had caught her attention. Wood cutouts of penguins wearing overalls² danced along the outside of the house. A sign below said, PENGUIN

---

2 overalls 상하의가 하나로 연결된 작업복.

Visits: $5. (Petting Extra. Market Pricing.[3])

"No penguins here anymore," their mother said, turning off the truck before **rummaging** through her bag. Her hand **emerged** with a **battered envelope**, which she shook until a single **tarnish**ed key dropped into her **palm**. "Are you ready to go check out our new home?"

"I wish there really were penguins inside," Nina **grumble**d. "That would make this move worth it."

Joel rubbed the top of her head. "I hear they're actually smelly and **cranky**. Maybe it's better that we just

---

3   market price 시장 가격. 상품이 시장에서 그때그때 실제적으로 거래되는 가격.

see them at the zoo, behind glass."

"They wouldn't be smelly and cranky to *me*," Nina **protest**ed. "We'd be friends!"

The kids followed their mother along the house's front path. **Fading** signs promised PENGUIN FEED: $2 and PENGUIN PORTRAITS: 4 FOR $4. "This was a penguin petting zoo," their mother explained. "The owners had hoped to make some money from the crowds that came to Stillwater each year to **celebrate** the Popper story. It's been a very long time since the original Popper Penguins lived in Stillwater, though, and even fewer people come to Hillport each year. The bank **foreclose**d the Penguin Pavilion, which is why I was able to **afford** it."

"And the Popper Penguins are part of your history, too, right?" Joel asked. "Which is why we have Popper as our last name?"

"In a way," she said. "But I'm a very **distant relation**. I never lived in Stillwater or Hillport, so this is as new to me as it is to you kids."

"What does 'foreclosed' mean?" Nina **whisper**ed to Joel, while their mother worked to fit the key into the lock.

"I think it means it was closed four times already," Joel said wisely. "That's what makes it cheap enough for Mom to afford."

The front door **creak**ed open. As soon as it did, Nina **raced** past, her voice **reverberating** through the halls. "I call this bedroom. No, wait, I call this one instead! You can have that first one!"

Joel didn't much care which room he got. He **hung back** near his mother, worried by how **drawn** she looked. It had been a very long drive through bad weather. "Here, Mom," he said, taking her heavy handbag from her and placing it on top of the **mantelpiece**. "Should I go start unpacking the truck?"

"We can do all that tomorrow," his mom said. She **pat**ted the bandanna[4] she always wore over her hair, **spatter**ed with paints from her latest **canvas**. She was a wonderful painter, though she could never seem to **settle on** any one subject. Some of the tiredness lifted from her eyes. "Nina has the right idea. Let's go **explore** the house!"

Then she was off, **track**ing **down** Nina. Joel closed the front door, made sure the dead **bolt**[5] was **secure**, then ran upstairs to join his mother and sister.

The house might have been cheap, but there was a

4　bandanna 반다나. 강한 햇빛을 가리거나 장식용 등으로 머리나 목에 두르는 얇은 천.
5　dead bolt 데드볼트. 주로 현관문에 사용되는 잠금장치의 일종으로 스프링 작용 없이 수동으로 열쇠를 돌려야만 작동하며, 열쇠 끝이 자물쇠의 판에 끼워지면서 문이 잠기거 나 열리게 되는 걸쇠 부분을 말한다.

reason. Its previous owners kept penguins here (which was, of course, **awesome**), but they had clearly not been into **housekeeping**. Even in the **dim reflect**ed light from the **streetlamps** outside, Joel could see the **grime** on the walls, and dust and **wrapp**ers **pile**d up in the corners. His mother stood in the middle of a **cramped** kitchen, already working on the **faucet**, which was **spray**ing out water. When she saw Joel, she gave a tight smile. "At least we know we have running water! Don't worry, we'll get this place cleaned up **in no time**."

"I'm sure we will, Mom," Joel said, **nodd**ing.

"Okay, this one is **definite**ly my room—no, wait, this one!" Nina **yell**ed from upstairs. "There's so many options!"

"You'd better go pick your own bedroom before your sister takes all of them," Mrs. Popper said.

Joel nodded and headed upstairs.

It was a quick choice. Joel let Nina pick whichever room made her happy and then selected the one next door to make life simple. "Come on, it's late and we've got a long day tomorrow," he said to his little sister. "We should go down and unpack our **sheet**s and toothbrushes, at least."

Nina **bound**ed down the stairs. "Ooh, look, a **basement**!"

"Let's go unpack, Nina!" Joel called down into the

dark. "We can explore the basement tomorrow."

"You have to see this!" she called up. "**Amazing!** Wow! Bring a flashlight!"

Grumbling, Joel un**clip**ped the flashlight from his belt (he was always prepared for **emergencies**) and headed down the creaking stairs. There were signs hanging from the **ceiling** above each step:

Get ready to pet!
Bundle up!
Penguin Pavilion main attraction!
Come meet penguins just
like Captain Cook and Greta!
Buy your tickets upstairs!

"This must be where they kept the penguins," he called to his sister as he stepped off the stairs and onto the cool, **dank** floor.

"Yes, definitely!" Nina said. "Let's take a look around."

Joel shone the flashlight around the walls. **Ice caps** and **glaciers** were painted on each surface, with rough **representation**s of penguins and **polar** bears[6] playing together in the **distance**. "Polar bears live in the **Arctic**," he said to Nina, "and penguins are in the *Antarctic*. Totally different **poles**. And they definitely wouldn't play together. Or wear these **silly** Santa hats."

"They're just paintings," Nina said, **poking around** the **edges** of the room. "I wish the penguins were still here. I've never met a penguin before."

Joel **sniffed**. "It still smells like birds. And old fish."

Nina took a big sniff, too. "I like the smell. Come here and shine the light on these gigant-o machines!"

Along one wall were what looked like big air conditioners. "These are probably how they kept the room cold."

"Do you think they turn on?" Nina asked.

"Of course they do. But we don't have any power," Joel replied, crossing his arms. "And we don't need to **freeze** this room if there are no penguins in it anymore. Electricity is expensive."

Nina disappeared around the back of one of the cooling **devices**. "There's a space back here. I can almost fit—wait, what's that? Whoa, I almost **crushed** it!"

"Crushed what?" Joel asked, shining the flashlight on his sister. He couldn't see what she'd found, though.

---

6 polar bear 북극곰. 몸의 길이는 2~2.5미터이며, 온몸에 순백색의 털이 촘촘히 나 있고 코, 입술, 발톱은 검은 색이다. 헤엄을 잘 치며 주로 북극 지방에 산다.

Her body was casting a shadow over it.

"**Hold on**—there's another one!" Nina turned around, with something in each hand.

"What are those?" Joel asked.

She worked her way out from behind the coolers. She was **speechless** as she lifted her hands up into the light.

It was very unusual for Nina to be speechless.

But in an **instant**, Joel could see why.

Cradled in each hand was an egg. They were grayish and **faintly speckled** and too big to be chicken eggs.

They had to be penguin eggs.

NINA AND JOEL BUILD A NEST

"KIDS?" MRS. POPPER asked from the top of the basement stairs. "What's going on down there?"

"Nothing!" Joel called up brightly. He whispered furiously in Nina's ear. "Put those eggs back."

"Why?" Nina protested. "We're going to love these eggs and maybe sit on them and hatch them, and then we'll have penguins!"

"Mom has enough to trouble her without also

worrying about the penguin eggs in our basement," Joel whispered.

"Are you **kid**ding? Mom will be excited, too! She loves animals."

"She might make us send them off to whatever zoo the Penguin **Pavilion** birds **wound up** in," Joel said. "We wouldn't want that, would we?"

That quieted Nina down. She shook her head **sober**ly.

To be honest, Joel wasn't sure what they should do next. He just knew he didn't like any unexpected **complication**s in his life, and this was **definite**ly an unexpected complication. At least these penguin eggs would probably never hatch. In any case, a few more hours in a corner of the basement wouldn't change their **fate**. He'd **debate** about what they should do overnight and then **come up with** a plan in the morning when he was thinking more clearly.

"Kids?" their mom called down. "Is everything okay?"

"Yes, fine!" Nina called as she carefully returned the eggs to their hiding place. She gave Joel a thumbs-up[1] and winked. Only she hadn't really learned how to wink yet, so it was more like an **exaggerate**d eye **scrunch**.

---

1 thumbs-up 주먹을 쥔 상태에서 엄지손가락만 세우는 동작으로, 만족이나 찬성의 뜻을 나타낼 때 사용한다.

Joel didn't sleep much that night. He lay in his strange new bed, looking out at the orange **streetlight** that shone through the broken **slat**ted **blind**s of his room, and considered his options.

By morning, he was pretty sure he had a **workable** plan.

At breakfast, he and Nina sat in a corner of the kitchen, cereal bowls in their **lap**s (they hadn't unpacked any tables and chairs yet). Their mother was in the bathroom, trying to un**clog** the toilet. It wasn't going well—they kept hearing **grunt**s and strange **gurgling** sounds. Joel didn't **dare peek** into the bathroom to see what was going on.

Gloop. Joel coughed. "Mom, Nina and I have to go to our new school on Monday, as you, um, as you know, of course, but did you know they sent a letter to our old house about what we needed to read for class?" *Glork.* "Well, they did, and I **memorize**d it, so, um, I was wondering if Nina and I could go to the library we passed on the way in and get out the books we need. It's just a couple of **block**s, and we'll be right back, you'll **barely** miss us? I'm sure the librarian will be nice and give us a card." *Glup.*

"Sure," their mother called **absent**ly. *Glip.* "You're old enough. I'll have this fixed by the time you're back." *Glook.*

Joel and Nina were already **halfway** out the front door,

pulling their shoes and jackets on. They dressed as they ran, **hop**ping until they had all four shoes on all four feet. "We're looking up how to care for penguin eggs, aren't we?" Nina said excitedly.

Joel **nod**ded and held open the library door for his sister. Once they were inside, Joel and Nina went straight back to the **reference section**, avoiding the curious **gaze** of the librarian. They didn't want anyone asking difficult questions.

"Penguins are 598.47," Joel said. "I hope that's a low shelf."

"How do you know the Dewey **Decimal** number[2] for penguins?" Nina asked.

"I remember **stuff**, I don't know," Joel said. "Here we go!"

Joel sat on the floor, legs crossed, and pulled books into his lap. "Okay, eggs in the index,[3] page twelve, here we go. **Incubation** temperature is 96.5 degrees.[4]"

"That's really hot, right?" Nina asked.

Joel nodded. "It's been a hot September, but not that

2　Dewey Decimal Number 듀이 십진분류법. 미국의 멜빌 듀이(Melvil Dewey)가 처음으로 만든 도서 분류법. 도서를 주제별로 0~9까지의 열 개 기초류로 나누고, 그 아래에 열 개의 강(綱)과 목(目)을 두어 모든 것을 아라비아 숫자로 적는 방법이다.

3　index 색인. 책 속의 내용 중에서 중요한 단어나 항목, 인명 등을 쉽게 찾아볼 수 있도록 일정한 순서에 따라 별도로 배열하여 놓은 목록.

4　96.5 degrees 화씨온도 96.5도는 섭씨온도 35.8도를 말한다.

hot. We need to get those eggs some heat. I hope it's not too late."

"There was probably heat coming out the back of the machines, back when power was on," Nina said. She flipped open her own penguin book and sounded out the captions[5] under the photographs. "'The parents take turns in . . . in . . . incubating the eggs.' I guess the little chicks inside like the feeling of being sat on. We should sit on them, too."

Joel snapped his fingers. "Hot-water bottles! We have some from when we were sick last winter."

"'Sometimes penguin parents wind up being two boys or two girls,'" Nina read out loud. "'Other penguins will adopt eggs if the original parent goes missing.' That's so sweet."

"Anything else? We should get back and warm those eggs. I wish we could bring the books with us, but of course they won't give library cards to kids without an adult present."

"I don't know why Mom didn't think of that," Nina said.

"She's an *artiste*," Joel replied. "That means she doesn't bother about small things." Like having the

---

5 caption 캡션. 도서 속 삽화나 사진 등에 붙는 짧은 설명이나 해설.

power turned on before they arrived at their new home.

Joel started re**shelving** the books. "Get your coat on, Nina."

"I didn't even take mine off!" Nina said.

"Oh," Joel said, **pat**ting his chest, "I didn't, either!"

Back at the house, Joel **rush**ed into the kitchen, while Nina went to **rummage** the hot-water bottles out of the moving truck. "How's the toilet going, Mom?" Joel called.

"Good!" she replied from the bathroom. "All unclogged. I took a moment to set up the **goldfish** tank, and now I'm working on the shower **drain**."

"Great. Say, I'm going to heat water . . . um, for tea.

Do you want some?"

Mrs. Popper **duck**ed into the kitchen, **wiping** her **brow**, a **confused** expression on her face. "You're making *tea?* Since when have you liked tea?"

"Yeah, um, I heard all the kids here in Hillport and Stillwater like tea. So I thought I'd try it out. I'd have something to talk about in the cafeteria, you know, to make myself some friends on my first day."

"Aww, honey," his mom said, coming over to give him a hug. "You'll make friends **in no time**. I'm sure of it. You're just the loveliest boy."

"So how does this work?" Joel asked, **fiddling** with the **knob**s on the **stove** top.

"It's gas, which luckily wasn't shut off," his mother said. "Here." The stove top **click**ed, and blue flames came out of a burner.

"Wow, fire," Joel said. "Let's make lots of hot water, because I want, um, lots and lots of tea!"

"Okay, okay," his mother said **distract**edly, filling a **kettle** with water from the **sink**. "After you drink your tea and do your reading for Monday, I'll need your and your sister's help. I want to give that front hall a good **scrub**."

"Sounds good," Joel said, **staring** at the **bead**s of water forming on the sides of the kettle.

Right then Nina came through the front door, an empty hot-water bottle in either hand. "Got 'em!"

"What did you unpack those for?" their mother asked.

"I just like the **comfort**ing feel," Nina replied, pressing the **rubber** against her cheek.

Mrs. Popper **narrow**ed her eyes.

"You know," Joel added **hastily**, "must be new-school **jitters**."

"You poor kids," their mother said. "This will be the last new school you ever have to go to, I promise."

"I can handle heating the water from here," Joel said. "Then we'll go do our reading."

"I want to do my reading in the basement!" Nina said.

Joel nodded **rapid**ly. "That's a great idea, Nina."

"Are you kids sure you're okay?" their mother asked, pressing her hand against Joel's **forehead**.

Nina **bound**ed down the steps into the basement. "Yep, totally! We're great! See you down here once you're ready, Joel!"

"**Study hall** is in **session**!" Joel said a few minutes later as he **race**d down after her with two hot-water bottles in hand. He hoped they wouldn't be too late.

OORK!

IT WAS THEIR first day of school, and Joel and Nina were taking a very long time getting their book bags ready. There were the usual folders and pencil cases and notebooks to **color-code** and arrange, of course, but there were also secret extra items: fleece[1] blankets, hot-water

---

1 fleece 플리스. 양모의 길고 부드러운 털을 곱슬거리게 한 천이나 이와 같은 느낌을 주기 위해 솜털을 세워 부드럽게 만든 직물이다. 보온성이 높아 주로 코트용 옷감으로 쓰인다.

bottles, and penguin eggs, one for each backpack.

"What's taking you kids so long?" their mother asked from the front **doorway**. "You don't want to be late on your first day!"

Joel and Nina **gingerly** noodled² their arms into their shoulder **straps**, one at a time. "Gently, gently," Joel said as they **tiptoed** toward the front door.

"What is wrong with you two?" their mother asked, **concern** on her face as her children **crept** toward her.

"Oh, you know, first-day **jitters**," Nina said.

"My dear little ones," Mrs. Popper said. "You'll have friends **in no time**. I'll walk you there and make sure you get in okay, too."

"No, thanks, Mom," Joel said quickly. "It's only a few **blocks** away. You took us on that practice run last night. We'll be fine."

"Okay then," she replied, her expression turning **wistful**. "I'll be right here once the school day's over. I'll want to hear every detail."

"Sounds good, bye, Mom!" Joel said as he and Nina tiptoed out the door. Their mother raised an **eyebrow** at them, then they were on the **sidewalk**.

---

2   noodle 단어 'noodle(밀가루로 만든 면 또는 국수)'은 주로 명사로 쓰이지만, 여기에서는 면의 구불구불한 모습에 빗대어 주인공이 조심스럽게 팔을 구부려 가방끈 안으로 집어 넣는 모습을 표현하기 위한 동사로 사용했다.

28

Did Joel feel a **nudge** inside his backpack? Was that possible?

After arriving at school, they parted ways to go to their **separate** homerooms, Joel to fifth grade and Nina to third. Joel moved so carefully through the **hallway**s that he was the last kid to arrive in his room. After **greet**ing him, Mrs. Mosedale placed him in the back row. "I'm seating you next to Michael," she said. "He'll be your guide for the day. Michael, you'll take good care of our new classmate, won't you?"

"Of course I will," Michael said, his face **beam**ing a little too much. He patted Joel on the shoulder, as if they were already friends. "I'll make sure our new buddy knows exactly where he belongs."

For some reason, Joel didn't get a good feeling about Michael. Not at all.

The day started with math, and while Mrs. Mosedale **demonstrate**d how to **multiply decimal**s, Joel's mind **wander**ed. How were Nina and her egg **faring** in her class? Then he started thinking about the penguin egg in his own backpack. He'd checked on it all weekend. It was almost killing him now not to be able to look at it.

"Mrs. Mosedale?" he asked, raising his hand once she'd **assign**ed them a set of exercises. "Could I go use the bathroom?"

"Of course. Take the hall pass," she said. "Michael, please show Joel the way."

"Sure, Mrs. Mosedale!" Michael said, beaming again. "I'll take him right there." His brightness felt cold, like a **fluorescent** bulb.

Joel **gripp**ed the straps of his backpack and stood.

"You don't need to bring your bag to the bathroom, new kid," Michael said **sharply.**

"I'd like to," Joel said, and hurried out of the classroom.

"You're **weird**," Michael said flatly as soon as the door closed. "No one brings their bag to the bathroom."

"I do," Joel said.

"Okay, whatever," Michael said. "The bathroom is down that hall. I'll wait here. I'm not going in with you." Joel could feel Michael's eyes against his back as he **cautious**ly **made his way** down the hallway.

As soon as he was in the bathroom, Joel **dipp**ed into a **stall** and opened the backpack. The egg was still there, **nestle**d safely in a fleece blanket and warmed by the hot-water bottle. He pulled the egg out. It was so *perfect*. He knew from his reading that its shape made it almost **indestructible**, even though it was protected by only a thin **layer** of calcium.[3] It could survive the worst storms

---

3   calcium 칼슘. 알칼리 토금속 원소의 하나로 무르고 은회색을 띠며, 동물의 뼈와 이에 주로 함유되어 있다. 여러 해양 생물들은 이것을 껍질 등을 만드는데 사용한다.

of **Antarctica** yet could also be opened from the inside by a weak baby chick. How **amazing**!

He **flush**ed the toilet, even though he hadn't done anything. Egg in his hand, he opened the stall door—and ran right into Michael.

"What is that?" Michael said, blocking the exit. "Give it to me, I want to see."

"**No way**," Joel said.

Joel went to put the egg back in the backpack, but before he could, Michael **snatch**ed it from his hands. "What is this? Is it from a dinosaur or something?"

"Give it back!" Joel said, **lunging** for it.

"No way. This is *awesome*. Everyone's going to love it!" Michael said. With that, he turned and ran.

"No, you'll hurt it! And it needs to stay warm!" Joel cried as he ran after Michael. The thought of the poor baby chick **jostling** inside, a **defense**less little animal that had already been through so much, brought tears to his eyes. Joel ran out of the bathroom and down the hallway.

Michael was *fast*. It was all Joel could do to keep him in view as he raced down the school's unfamiliar **corridors**. **Startled** kids **peer**ed out of the windows of the classrooms they passed. All it would take was one teacher coming out into the hallway, and it would all be over. The egg would be **confiscated**.

Michael **toss**ed the egg in the air as he ran, shouting **taunt**s behind him. "You want it back? How much do you want it back?"

"Stop it!" Joel **yell**ed.

Michael **slam**med through some double doors, and suddenly they were out on the playground, running across the **stretch** of open asphalt[4] between two basketball **hoop**s. Not too far away, a group of little kids was playing four square.[5] Their teacher was busy taking **roll call**. No one had **notice**d the egg—yet.

Michael tossed the egg high in the air and **barely** caught it, **diving** for it with both hands **extend**ed. Then he tossed the egg right into the air again.

"Give it back!" Joel called as he **rush**ed toward Michael, reaching his arms out to **beat** him to the falling egg. Like outfielders[6] after a fly ball,[7] they **stare**d up at the sky at the egg turning end over end. It passed in front of the sun, and they were both **blind**ed. The boys **knock**ed into each other. Seeing purple, Joel **flail**ed his hands through

---

4   asphalt 아스팔트. 석유를 정제할 때 잔류물로 얻어지는 고체 또는 반고체의 검은색이나 흑갈색 탄화수소 화합물. 도로포장, 방수, 또는 방습의 재료로 쓴다.

5   four square 포 스퀘어. 사분면으로 나뉘어진 사각형의 코트 위에 네 명의 사람들이 각 구역에 서서 서로 공을 퉁겨 주고받는 놀이.

6   outfielder 외야수. 야구에서 외야를 수비하는 좌익수, 우익수, 그리고 중견수를 통틀어 이르는 말.

7   fly ball 플라이 볼. 야구에서 타자가 공을 하늘 높이 쳐 올린 상태나 그 공을 말한다.

32

the air, hoping to make contact with the egg.

But he didn't. All he heard was a loud **crack**.

Furious, he **shove**d Michael away. "No!"

At Joel's feet were **ruins** of **eggshell**, gray on the outside and **brilliant** white on the inside. In the middle was a wet little bird, no bigger than a **fist**. It was on its side, but then it righted itself and looked directly at Joel. It **flap**ped its **miniscule** wings, opened and closed its **beak**. Then it made a sound. *"Oork!"*

A POP QUIZ

NINA'S QUIZ WAS not going well. If only they had
started with math, then she would have been right on
top of it. Spelling **was unfortunately** *not* **her strong suit**. It
wasn't fair—she was new, which meant she hadn't had
a chance to study any of these words! Mr. Prendergast
said just to do her best, and the grade wouldn't **count**,
but even so, Nina took an extra moment to **curse** being
the new kid again. It was the **absolute** worst.

How did anyone know how to spell *wrinkle*? Nina had an *r* down on her paper, but it already didn't look right.

She spared a moment to glance down at her bag, which she'd left open at the side of her desk—quite cleverly, she thought. She could check on the egg all through class. It was nestled snugly in its fleece blanket, heat radiating up from the hot-water bottle, enough to turn Nina's forehead sweaty.

Wait—did the egg have a crack in it?

"Eyes on your paper, Nina," Mr. Prendergast said.

"Sorry," Nina said, returning to *wrinkle*. Her face flushed even more. He thought she'd been cheating! This was not going to be a good first impression.

"The next word," Mr. Prendergast said, "is 'content,' as in 'satisfied.' 'Content.' "

Nina spent a long time penciling a *c*, sneaking glances at her bag. The egg was definitely shaking, and the crack was getting bigger. She could hear a tapping sound. She scratched her pencil harder along her paper, hoping that the sound would cover the ones coming from the egg.

Oh my! There was a *hole* in the egg now, and from the other side of the hole emerged a little beak, hard and black and with a hook on the end. Nina knew from her library research that that was called an egg tooth.[1] The chick was coming out! She wished Joel were here to see. Some situations just **called for** a big brother.

She had only one letter down again when Mr. Prendergast called out the next word. *Highway.* This one Nina had a better chance on.

She just let her pencil make random movements on the paper, though, while she stared down at the chick. It was fully out of its **shell** now. A real live baby penguin! Oh my gosh!

Then it made its first noise: A very small *oork!* The student on Nina's right looked up and around, **confused**.

Uh-oh. This was going to **get out of hand** very quickly.

"Oork, oork!"

Before Nina could stop it, the chick picked its way out of the shell, then up and out of her backpack and onto the classroom floor. "No, stop!" she whispered as the bird started **toddling** under her desk, holding out its **flippers**. It was very cute, a dark gray ball of **fuzz** with a white **belly** and sleepy black eyes. But cuteness wouldn't be enough to keep the bird from getting both of them into trouble very quickly.

"'**Nectar**,'" Mr. Prendergast called out as the chick gave the leg of Nina's desk an **experimental peck**.

---

1 egg tooth 난치(卵齒). 조류나 파충류 등의 새끼가 부화될 때 알 속의 새끼에게 돋아나는, 알을 깨부수기 위한 단단한 돌기 모양의 구조.

Nina **slunk** down in her desk, **slip**ped onto the floor, and got up on her hands and **knees**.

What are you doing? the girl next to her **mouth**ed.

Nina reached her hands around the chick. It was so **fragile** and light, bits of egg still stuck to its feathers. The chick disappeared entirely in Nina's hands. It felt like holding a Christmas **ornament**. Nina **eased** back into her chair, hands **cup**ping the baby penguin. It pecked at Nina's **palms**. It **tickled**.

"Is everything okay, Nina?" Mr. Prendergast asked, looking over at her.

Nina nodded **emphatic**ally.

As Mr. Prendergast called out "'**Adapt**,'" Nina **delicate**ly lowered her hands into her backpack and **release**d the chick. Before it could get out again, she **zip**ped the bag shut.

She could still hear the chick making its **squeaky** *oork* sounds inside. The girl next to her had given up on her quiz and was staring at Nina's shaking backpack with **astonish**ment. This situation was soon going to . . . what was the word . . .

"'**Escalate**,'" Mr. Prendergast called.

Yep! **That was it!**

Nina had just written an *e* down on her paper when Joel appeared at the classroom door. He looked sweaty and **out of breath**, wearing his backpack on his front. If Nina wasn't mistaken, Joel's bag was shaking, too.

"Can I help you, young man?" asked Mr. Prendergast, clearly **irritated** at the **interrupt**ion.

"I'm sorry," Joel said. "My name is Joel Popper. Nina is my sister, and I have to go home sick. Our mother is on the way. The front office said I could come get Nina, so we could go home together."

"Are you sure? That's most unusual," Mr. Prendergast said, folding his arms over his sweater vest.

Nina looked from her brother to Mr. Prendergast, her mind racing. Then she coughed. Her hand was already reaching for her backpack. "Yes, I'm feeling sick, too!"

ERNEST AND MAE

"KIIIIDS," MRS. POPPER said as she walked them home, "are you *sure* that you're both sick?"

"Yes, of course we are," Joel said quickly.

Nina coughed **pointed**ly.

Their mother was carrying their backpacks for them, which she always did when they weren't feeling well. Joel watched the bags to see if the **chick**s were moving. But they weren't, and he couldn't hear any *oorks*. Maybe the chicks had fallen asleep.

Mrs. Popper chose her words carefully. "I wonder if maybe you two were **overwhelm**ed by your first day, and you called out sick because you wanted to come home."

Nina coughed again, shaking her head at the same time.

Joel always felt terrible whenever he lied, so he took the opportunity to clear his **conscience**. "Yeah, that might have been it, Mom. We just wanted to come home."

Nina stopped coughing.

"I wish you had told me the truth from the start."

Nina took their mother's hand in hers and **squeeze**d. "Sorry, Mom. They might not have called you if we didn't say we were sick."

Mrs. Popper **ruffle**d Nina's hair. "I know this move is hard on you both. None of us expected your father to leave, that I'd have to find a way to **get by** on one **income**. But we have a house we can call ours now. We *own* it. Everything is going to be different from here on out."

"I **bet** you're right, Mom," Joel said. "That sounds nice."

"I love you two," Mrs. Popper said.

"Do we have any tuna fish?" Joel asked.

"Oh!" Mrs. Popper said, surprised. "We . . . *do* have tuna fish."

As soon as they were inside, Joel and Nina **dashed** upstairs and **huddle**d in Nina's room, where they un**zip**ped their backpacks and **peer**ed in.

"Oh, thank God," Joel said as he pulled his chick out. It sat on his palm quietly, peering up at him with its deep, dark eyes.

"Mine's okay, too!" Nina cried. Her chick was far more **energetic, hop**ping out of her hand and **wander**ing around the room, checking out the corners, *oork*ing away. Nina **sigh**ed. "It's so cute!"

"It is. They both are," Joel said, lowering his chick to the ground. It **chase**d after Nina's, and once it'd **caught up**, it huddled against the other penguin, little **fuzzy** wing reaching out for **comfort**. They both kept *oork*ing. "I bet they're hungry."

"I'll go get the tuna fish," Nina said, and ran downstairs.

Joel **kneel**ed on the floor. Tears of joy filled his eyes while he watched the chicks. They were so perfect. Then he **leap**ed to his feet. The penguins were heading right out of the bedroom! Joel shut the door just **in time**, before the chicks wandered out into the **hallway**. They hit the wood and turned around. The **startled** chicks *oork*ed even louder. Two baby penguins were going to be a lot of work.

"Here, you two," Joel said, lying on his **stomach** so he was eye level with them. "Come say hi."

The penguins **waddle**d over **awkward**ly, passing right by Joel's head and **wedging** into the space between his neck and the floor, one on either side. Joel laughed. "You guys want to feel like you're under an adult penguin's **belly**, don't you?"

"Oork! Oork!"

Fuzzy feathers **tickle**d Joel's throat. It was all he could manage not to laugh out loud.

The door **creak**ed open. Joel didn't want to **disturb** the **nest**ing penguins, so he didn't **dare** look up to see who was coming in. He was **relieved** to see Nina's sneakers coming toward him, not his mother's loafers.[1]

Nina set down a plate of tuna fish. "We're lucky Mom is so **distract**ed by moving in," she said. "She didn't even **notice** I was making a plate of plain tuna. Come on, birds, it's lunchtime!"

The chicks **wriggle**d out from under Joel's throat. They waddled over to the plate, brought their eyes close to the fish, then looked up at Nina and Joel **expectant**ly.

"What are they waiting for?" Joel asked.

"In the books from the library, it looked like the parents **fed** the chicks."

"I don't remember that part. How do they feed them?

---

1 loafer 로퍼. 버클이나 끈이 없어 신고 벗기가 편하고 굽이 낮은 신발.

It's not like penguins have hands to hold fish."

"No, they . . . you know, **regurgitate**." Nina opened her mouth and did a very believable **impression** of **vomit**ing.

"**Gross**."

Nina picked up a piece of tuna and **dangle**d it over the chicks' heads. They opened their mouths and **bounced**. *"Oork! Oork!"* She dropped the **morsel** into one mouth, and the chick happily **gum**med it down.

Joel sat up, selected a piece of tuna, and dropped it into the other chick's mouth. That bird, too, eagerly **swallow**ed the food.

"We should call them Hungry and Eat-y," Nina **propos**ed.

"The Popper Penguins were named after famous travelers," Joel said. "We don't know if these are boys or girls yet, but what if we named them Ernest, for Ernest Shackleton, who went to the South **Pole**, and . . . and—"

"Mae, for Mae Jemison!" Nina said. "She went to space."

"Perfect."

"That'll be the more energetic one. Your shyer one can be Ernest."

Joel picked Ernest up and looked into his eyes. "You can be as shy as you want. We'll take good care of you."

"Kids!" their mother called from downstairs. "You promised to help me, since you're not actually sick!"

"We'll take these two down to the **basement** and then go help Mom," Joel **whispered**.

They each **scoop**ed a chick into their T-shirts and **hustle**d downstairs.

They opened the basement door—which **squeak**ed. "Kids, now! I'm not **messing around**," their mom called.

"Sorry, Mom!" They **deposit**ed the chicks, their fleece blankets, hot-water bottles, and tuna fish in the middle of the basement floor, then **race**d upstairs.

As Joel closed the basement door, all he could hear were the **bewilder**ed *oorks* of the chicks.

"I don't think we'll be able to **pull** this **off** for too long," Nina whispered to Joel as they rushed toward their mother.

"I don't know if we'll be able to pull it off for a *day*," Joel replied.

It would turn out to be closer to ten minutes.

THE WAY OF ALL GOLDFISH

THE FIRST TASK of the day was to finish unloading the moving truck so their mother could return it. Each time Joel went to get a box, he tried to pick one that was labeled BASEMENT, so he could check on Ernest and Mae. But Mrs. Popper wasn't playing along. "We should save the basement boxes for the end, kids. That's the last priority. Start with the bedroom stuff, so we can get this house feeling like a home."

"If only she knew," Nina said **under her breath** as she **dragg**ed a floor lamp through the front door, passing right under the old Penguin Pavilion sign.

Joel put his hands on his **hip**s and looked around the moving truck. "Mom, where'd you **wind up** putting the goldfish?"

"Winkles and Joffrey?" she said, **wiping** her **brow.** "I think it might have been the basement."

Joel nearly dropped the box he was holding. "You put them in the basement?" He ran out of the truck and into the house. "Nina! The goldfish are in the basement!"

"So what?" Nina said. Then she saw Joel's **horrified** expression. "Oh! The basement!"

They threw open the door and ran down the steps.

They were just **in time** to see the goldfishes' **tails** disappear down the penguin's open beaks, one in each. *Slurp, slurp.*

"Oork, oork!"

The chicks waddled forward and back, turning in circles and raising their little wings, clearly pleased with themselves.

Nina stood **openmouthed.** "Goodbye, Winkles."

Joel put his arm around her shoulders. "Goodbye, Joffrey."

Emboldened, Mae hopped up onto the first step and then the second. Ernest looked at Mae in **wonderment**, then tried to hop onto the first step. It didn't go nearly as well. He hit the step mid-belly and then fell back to the floor, **astonish**ed. *"Oork! Oork!"* he cried.

Joel **rush**ed to **cradle** him, while Nina played **defense**, positioning her feet along a step to prevent Mae from jumping any higher, looking just like a soccer **goalie** trying to **block** a shot.

Mae might have been only a few hours old, but she was already clever. She waddled left on her step and then took a surprise waddle to the right before jumping,

skirting right by Nina.

Then Mae was up and out of the basement door and into the rest of the house.

"Oh no, oh no," Nina cried as she **scrambled** after the fast-moving chick.

The baby penguin was already in the kitchen, **peck**ing at the corner of a cardboard[1] moving box, when Nina **caught up** to her. She **scoop**ed up the **cuddly** little chick. "You have to stay in the basement, **naughty** Mae!"

Nina heard a loud **gasp**. She turned and nearly dropped the chick in surprise.

There, mouth open in a wide O of astonishment, was Mrs. Popper.

---

1 cardboard 판지. 두껍고 단단하게 널빤지 모양으로 만든 종이.

GROUNDED?

IT WAS A very **somber** family meeting. Or it would have been a very somber family meeting, if two penguin chicks hadn't been wandering around the dining room table. Mae and Ernest *oork*ed with **curiosity**, frequently lifting their wings up and down until someone **cuddled** them.

"I cannot *believe* that you kids thought it was okay to lie to me," Mrs. Popper was saying. She had to **break off**, though, when Ernest stood in front of her and fixed her with an **intense stare**. "What do *you* want?"

"He wants you to hold him," Joel explained.

Mrs. Popper nervously picked up the chick and **cradle**d him in the **crook** of her **elbow**. Her expression **melt**ed. "Is that better, Ernest? Anyway, what was I saying, oh, right, I'm very mad at you for thinking you could lie to your very own mother—what do you want? Are you hungry, little Ernest? Aww!"

"They really love tuna fish," Nina said quietly.

"Well, we should **stock up**," Mrs. Popper said. "We have only a couple of cans left." She **struggle**d to turn her expression **stern** again. "This doesn't mean that I'm okay with your lying to me. You two are still in big trouble."

Joel **nod**ded **solemn**ly. "Yes. Big trouble. Got it."

"We didn't want you to send them to the zoo!" Nina **wail**ed.

"We think they should live with *us*," Joel **clarified**.

"They can*not* live with us," Mrs. Popper said. "That's not **negotiable**. Penguins do not belong in houses."

"The Poppers did it!" Nina said.

"That was a long time ago," Mrs. Popper said. "And what happened in the end? They realized that the penguins needed to be in nature, and Mr. Popper did the right thing. He brought them back to the wild."

"Mom?" Joel said.

"Yes, Joel?"

"The Penguin Pavilion was already closed when we got here, so I didn't see it in action or anything, but I don't think it sounds like it was a good place for penguins. They left two eggs behind! I don't think they deserve to have Ernest and Mae back."

Their mother sighed. "I'm inclined to agree. Also, I don't know where they are. The Penguin Pavilion left in the middle of the night, without telling anyone where they were going. They owed a lot of money and just disappeared."

Through with cuddles for the moment, Ernest thrashed until Mrs. Popper released him onto the table. He waddled over to the edge and sniffed the air, beak pointing toward the kitchen. He had clearly decided it was time to eat again. As if to make a point, he deposited a bright white smear of penguin poo on the tabletop.

"I'll clean that up!" Joel said hurriedly.

As a parent, Mrs. Popper found a smear of poo was no big deal. Without missing a beat, she pulled a handkerchief out of her back pocket and wiped it away.

"Does that mean we're *not* bringing them to the zoo? But you also said they couldn't stay here. I guess I'm confused," Nina said.

"I'm a little confused, too," Mrs. Popper confessed. She'd always been very honest with her children. "These penguins belong in the wild, but we can't exactly bring them to the local beach, can we? They need a *cold* wilderness."

Joel thought for a long moment. "Every kid around here knows that Mr. Popper brought his penguins up to the Arctic, to Popper Island," he said. "What if we brought these chicks up to live with them?"

Nina hooted. "That would be amazing!"

Never one to be left out, Mae gave an excited *oork* from where she was nestled in Nina's arms.

"It's fall break soon," Nina said, petting Mae's fuzzy head. "We could go then!"

"Just how do you kids imagine we'll get all the way to the Arctic?" Mrs. Popper asked.

"Stillwater might be the fancier city," Joel said, "but there's one advantage to living in Hill*port*, if you catch my drift."

"I have no idea what you're talking about," Nina said.

"Port, Nina, *port*," he said, pantomiming a ship rocking on the sea.

"Oh, yay!" Nina said. "I do like traveling by boat!"

THE POPPER FOUNDATION

IT WAS ONLY their second day of school, and yet the Popper children had already accomplished so much. They'd hatched two penguin chicks and come up with a plan for how to find them a home. Nina had even learned her spelling words—she wasn't going to repeat *that* disaster again!

While the kids were in school, they left their chicks under the watchful eye of Mrs. Popper. As Ernest and Mae napped in the morning, Mrs. Popper went to the library to do some research of her own. She soon discovered that hatched birds don't need any special heat sources in a **temperate climate** like Hillport's—in fact their feathers **insulate**d them so well that, until winter came, they'd need a way to cool down!

She went to the grocery store and bought some big bags of ice, which she **dump**ed into a **shallow tub** in the corner of the kitchen. The penguins were smart creatures, she **figure**d, and could decide how cold they wanted to be, using the ice as much as they saw fit. And that's just what they did, **hop**ping into the tub to play in the cubes for a while before joining Mrs. Popper in unpacking dishes (a task at which they were **distinct**ly **unhelpful**), and then returning to the ice bath for some more cooling down.

As soon as the school day was over, the kids **bound**ed home to see their chicks. Ernest and Mae **greet**ed them with many **cheep**s and *oorks*. First the kids brought the chicks to the bathtub to swim **laps**. Then Joel lay on the floor, **belly**-down, and Ernest happily **burrow**ed under his throat, his **nesting** position. Nina and Mae did the same. "Could you get our schoolbags for us, Mom?" Nina asked. "We'd better get used to doing our homework in this position."

Mrs. Popper **retrieve**d their bags from where they'd

dropped them by the front door. "Once the penguins have had their snuggles and you've all had your afternoon snack, we'll go down to the port to visit the Popper Foundation and see what they can do to help put our plan into action."

"Really?" Joel said. "We're going to ask them to get us to Popper Island? All the way in the Arctic?"

"That will be the best fall break ever," Nina said.

"Can we bring Ernest and Mae to the port with us?" Joel asked once the snack was over.

"It does seem sad to leave them behind," Mrs. Popper said. "Yes, we'll bring them to the Popper Foundation, as long as you kids hold them tight."

Ernest and Mae seemed to enjoy the car trip, turning their heads to and fro so they could peer out with one eye and then the other. Joel was learning that they didn't face what they were looking at, usually, because of where their eyes were placed on their heads. Having an eye on either side allowed them to see all around them—which was probably very useful for avoiding seals in the water!

Once they'd parked at the harbor, Mrs. Popper led the kids to an address she'd written down on the back of an envelope. It was the office of the Popper Foundation. They knocked on a beautiful wooden door, carved with decorations of twelve regal-looking penguins.

The door buzzed open, and the Poppers filed into

the foundation's office.

"Sorry, busy today, come again another time," the foundation **representative** said without looking up from his desk. He was a **blustery bald** man, with dried sea salt on his **mustache**.

Mae cheeped in **outrage**. The representative looked up. "Oh! Penguins!"

"We have two penguins here that need to get to the wild," Nina said, sticking out her chest a **trifle** self-importantly. "And we're *Poppers*. **Distant relation**s."

"Penguins!" the representative behind the desk repeated, his face warming at the **sight** of the two fuzzy little chicks.

"We're hoping that we can bring these two to Popper Island, to live with the Popper Penguins!" Joel said.

"My understanding is that the only way to communicate with Popper Island is by **maritime** radio," Mrs. Popper said. "Could you try to ring them up for us, to ask if they might be able to pick these chicks up the next time they come to town for **supplies**?"

"I'll try," the representative said, **crack**ing his **knuckles**. "But it won't go well."

They all watched as he put on a headset and turned some dials. Even the chicks went silent, watching curiously from Nina's and Joel's arms. "Popper Island Station come

in, Popper Island Station come in." He removed the headset and turned back to them. "No answer. In fact, there's been no answer for months."

"Doesn't that **count** as an **emergency**?" Mrs. Popper asked, surprised.

"It's been **decade**s since Mr. Popper brought the original twelve penguins there, of course. The foundation pays a local guy to be the island's **caretaker** now. There wasn't a **distress signal**. Perhaps the caretaker left the penguins to run themselves for a few weeks. That's no **crisis in my book**."

"It could be a crisis for the penguins!" Nina said

hotly. "Mr. Popper would be outraged!"

"Won't there be an **investigation**?" Joel tried.

"I'm afraid there's nothing like that planned," the representative said.

The kids looked up at their mother. She crossed her arms, **knead**ing the **elbows** of her well-worn jacket. "Is there any other way to get to Popper Island? Someone needs to **figure out** if everything is okay. And get these two chicks up there."

The representative pulled out an **atlas**, laid it flat on his desk, and **beckon**ed them all to come around. Joel and Nina placed Mae and Ernest on top of the map. The chicks peered in wonder at the greens and blues beneath their feet.

The man with the mustache pointed at a small **blip** off the east coast of Canada. "That's Popper Island, see?" As he **gesture**d with his fingers, Mae took a curious **nip** at his wedding band. The **burly** representative ignored her as he **trace**d a path along the blue ink of the water. "This is where the fishing routes normally go. As you can see, none of them travel anywhere near."

The **kids' faces fell.**

"We have to find a way to get there," Mrs. Popper said **resolute**ly.

"Well, yes, madam," the representative said, smiling

for the first time that afternoon. "This is the Popper Foundation, and our purpose is to care for the Popper Penguins. We care a great deal." He scrawled a name and phone number down on a piece of paper. "Contact Yuka. He grew up near Popper Island and takes trips back up there sometimes to visit his family. He has a sturdy little boat and is an excellent captain. He'll get your penguins there safely. Of course, the Popper Foundation will fund the expedition, since you'll also be doing us the favor of reporting back on how the Popper birds are doing."

"*Oork!*" said Mae triumphantly, before taking another friendly nip at the representative's knuckle.

LEAVING HILLPORT

THE SMALL BOAT dipped and rocked where it was tied to the Hillport **dock**. "Are you sure this is **seaworthy**? I mean, *Arctic* seaworthy?" Joel **whisper**ed to his mother.

"This looks amazing!" Nina said, bounding **aboard**. She held Mae out in her **palm**s, turning in a circle. The chick peered up and down. *"Oork, oork!"* In just the last few weeks, her voice had changed some. Her *oorks* were getting closer to adult penguin *orks*.

"It's going to be totally safe," Mrs. Popper said as she stepped onto the **deck**. "Come on, kids, I want to introduce you to Yuka."

Joel and Nina brought their two chicks to Yuka. He was a young man with an open, **friendly** face.

"Hi there!" Yuka said. When he reached out his hand for a shake, Joel didn't know what to do at first and gave him his left hand, until he realized he should **switch** them, **awkward**ly **juggling** Ernest in the process. Nina, of course, **figured** **out** handshakes right away.

"Yuka is Inuit,[1]" Mrs. Popper explained. "That means his **ancestor**s lived in the Arctic long before Europeans

got there."

Yuka nodded. "It's been a few years since I lived up there, though. I came down to Stillwater College to get my **doctorate** in **comparative zoology**.[2] I study **aquatic** bird **migration**s, actually! That's why the Popper **Foundation** knew about me."

Ernest made an **impressed** *oork*. Joel was more **suspicious**. "So you're not actually a sailor?"

"I come from a long **line** of fishermen. This is my family's boat. It's a wonderful deep-sea fishing **vessel** and does fine in rough waters. Don't worry—I know how to handle the waterways. And I have a seminar paper due in a few weeks, so I'll make sure this is an **efficient** trip. You won't miss any school, and neither will I!"

"It's not like missing school would be *that* terrible," Nina said.

"We're very **grateful**, Yuka," Mrs. Popper said. "Thank you for taking this time."

"It's an **honor** to help these little guys," Yuka said. He **duck**ed his head to get a better look at the fuzzy gray chicks. "I like those pretty white **stripe**s on your

---

1 Inuit 이누이트. 북극, 캐나다, 그린란드 및 시베리아의 북극 지방에 사는 인종. 주로 수렵이나 어로에 종사하고, 여름에는 흩어져 살다가 겨울에는 집단으로 거주한다.

2 comparative zoology 비교 동물학. 여러 동물의 분류, 형태, 발생, 생태, 유전, 진화 등을 그 차이 또는 유사의 관점에서 비교 연구하는 생물학의 한 분야.

flippers!"

"*Oork! Oork!*" Ernest turned around so Yuka could see his coloring on all sides. He was turning out to be a vain little penguin.

Yuka tilted his head at Mrs. Popper. "You've got everything from the packing list we settled on?"

"Yes! Lots of warm, waterproof layers."

"And tuna fish!" Nina added.

"That's good," Yuka said. "This boat may still smell a little like fish, but it's been years since it did any fishing. I just use it to get back and forth to school. So it's good you're bringing your own food for the birds." He threw open the small hatch that led belowdecks. "Here are our quarters. Not too roomy, but I've always liked it down there. 'Homey' is probably the best word for it."

Joel peeked in. The cabin was clean and pleasant, with a fridge and a small stove top and neatly made bunks covered in red plaid sheets. A fine place to spend a week.

"I think we're ready to go!" Mrs. Popper said.

"All aboard!" Yuka called. He leaned down to confide in Joel. "I've always wanted to say that, but it would feel silly when I'm traveling alone."

Once the boat had been freed from the dock, Yuka started the engine. Before long, they were puttering out of Hillport harbor.

The kids placed their chicks on the deck. The penguins **waddle**d over to the edge, to **gaze** down at the water flowing past the boat. They'd taken to swimming laps in the ba**tub**, so Joel wasn't too worried about what would happen if they fell in. Yuka would just stop the boat and fish them out of the water. The chicks would be sure to enjoy the process **immensely**.

"Once we get up there," Nina whispered, "how are we going to say goodbye to Ernest and Mae?"

"We'll find a way," Joel said, putting an arm around his sister. "Being with other penguins is what's right for them."

Nina **kneel**ed at the edge of the deck. Mae **toddle**d over and hopped into her lap. "I guess. But it'll still be hard to say goodbye."

Not one to be **left out**, Ernest **pinch**ed the **fabric** of Nina's jeans with his beak and lifted himself into her lap. He was turning out to be a smaller penguin than his sister and sometimes needed help getting himself everywhere he wanted to go.

"I know it will be hard," Joel said, watching Ernest **snuggle** in closer to Nina. "I know it."

Ernest **let out** a long *oooork*. "Sounds like he knows it, too," Nina said.

"Actually, I think that just means he's ready for some more tuna fish."

THE JOURNEY BEGINS

JOEL LOVED SPENDING his day at the **helm** with Yuka. There were so many **instruments** and **panels** to **investigate**, and Yuka would often let him take control—while keeping **an eye out**, of course.

Sometimes Joel would catch his mother watching the two of them with an expression that looked both sad and happy. It wasn't hard to imagine where her thoughts were. Joel sometimes **overheard** his mother talking to her friends on her phone about how she was worried Joel didn't have any "male role models" in his life. But that was **ridiculous**. Joel wasn't excited to spend time with Yuka because he was a "male role model." It was all about the instruments and panels!

Nina would often want her turn, too, so they'd **switch** off, and Joel would take over minding the chicks. Mae and Ernest spent most of each day sleeping. At first Joel and Nina had been worried they were sick, but then Mrs. Popper pointed out that the chicks were probably sleeping so much because they were growing so fast. **Apparent**ly Joel and Nina had done the same thing

when they were babies.

When the chicks weren't sleeping, they made plenty of trouble. Ernest preferred to be at the **stern**. Sometimes he'd **poke around** the boat's engines, investigating the various **hum**ming **devices**. Other times he'd **stare** into the waves and **flap** his wings—Joel could imagine him preparing for the day when he'd be swimming through ocean water. Mae preferred to be **perch**ed at the **bow**, like the figurehead[1] on a pirate ship. Whichever kid was **on duty** would have to walk the **deck**, making sure that neither chick fell into the surf.

Chicks falling **overboard** wouldn't turn out to be the problem.

Yuka was an excellent sailor, **diligent**ly minding the controls even as he told **elaborate** tales about his childhood in the **Arctic**, complete with **impersonation**s of all his family members. On the fourth morning, though, he seemed **preoccupied**. He spent a long time examining his **atlas** after he pulled up **anchor**.

"This **makes** no **sense**," he said.

Mrs. Popper, Joel, and Nina crowded around Yuka. Not to be **left out**, Ernest and Mae *oork*ed until the kids picked them up so they could see what all the **fuss** was about.

---

1 figurehead 선수상. 배의 앞머리에 장식으로 붙이는 사람이나 동물의 상(像).

"All my **instrumentation** agrees that we're here," Yuka said, pointing to a **spot** on the map as the boat sped forward.

"That's good, right?" Nina said.

"Yes," Yuka said, **draw**ing **out** the word as he pointed at the **horizon**. "But if that's true, we wouldn't be here already."

"We wouldn't be *where* already?" Joel asked.

"Popper Island!"

"What?" Nina **yell**ed, jumping up and down.

"Careful with Mae," Joel **scold**ed. But the chick was clearly enjoying the action, her cries joining Nina's. Joel put a hand over his eyes, like a **visor**, and **squint**ed. They were approaching a **windswept pile** of dark gray rocks, sticking up out of the ocean. It looked **brutal** and **unforgiving** to Joel—but who knew, maybe it was paradise to a penguin's eyes.

"Are you sure that's Popper Island ahead of us?" Mrs. Popper asked.

Yuka **nod**ded. "**Definite**ly. I grew up around here, and I'd **recognize** those rock **formation**s anywhere."

"But how could all your instruments be wrong?" Nina asked.

"They're connected to a central computer on the boat," Yuka said. "If my **navigation** systems have us in the wrong position it really isn't good, because that means I don't have **readout**s on nearby undersea **obstacle**s. It's dangerous."

"Where is the computer **locate**d?" Joel asked with a **sink**ing feeling.

"At the stern."

Joel **slipp**ed away to the back of the boat, Ernest **chirp**ing happily once he realized they were heading to his favorite spot. He hopped down and examined the engine like usual before sitting and **gazing** into the water.

Joel **spied** the computer, housed in a plastic box on the floor. He'd never **bother**ed to look closely at it before. A corner had been **bent** away, the contents **dragged** out onto the deck. Some **wires**, some transistors,[2] some microchips.[3] Right in front of Joel's eyes, Ernest reached in with his **beak**, pulled out another microchip, toddled to the **edge** of the boat, and **pitch**ed it over. He watched happily as it dropped into the **rush**ing waves, then looked up at Joel with pride. *"Oork!"*

"Oh no!" Joel yelled, hands on his cheeks. "Yuka,

---

2 transistor 트랜지스터. 전류나 전압의 흐름을 조절하여 증폭하거나 스위치 역할을 하는 반도체 소자. 외부 회로와 연결할 수 있는 세 개 이상의 전극을 가지고 있다.

3 microchip 마이크로칩. 아주 작은 실리콘 칩 표면에 수천 개의 전자 요소와 회로 패턴을 수용하고 있는 반도체 부품.

Ernest's been **meddling** with the computer!"

There was no answer from the helm. Joel ran up there to find Yuka **grip**ping the wheel with white **knuckles**,[4] Mrs. Popper and Nina standing beside him. "What's going—"

"There!" Yuka shouted, pointing at a dark shape in the water, passing under the **prow**. "That's the rocks—hold on tight!"

Joel was **interrupt**ed by a horrible **grind**ing sound from the **hull**. The whole **vessel** slowed, and the bow **dipp**ed, pitching them all forward. They **barely** caught themselves at the **railing**, Mae tight in Nina's hand, narrowly missing getting **pin**ned against the rail.

At first it felt like the boat might **tip over** and **cast** them into the sea. The back rose **alarming**ly, then **crash**ed back into the ocean. The engines continued to **roar**, but the boat didn't move forward anymore. It just ground against the undersea rocks.

While Yuka **frantic**ally **man**ned the helm, throwing **levers** and pushing buttons to cut the engines before the boat **tore** itself apart, Joel **raced** to the stern. He could just imagine Ernest cast into the sea, falling toward the propeller **blade**s below. "Ernest!"

---

4 white knuckle 겁에 질리거나 긴장하여 손을 꼭 움켜쥘 때 손가락 관절이 하얗게 변하는 모습에서 유래된 표현으로, 아주 긴장하거나 겁먹은 상태를 나타내는 표현.

The chick was toddling toward him. Joel **scooped** him up, **relieved**. As he did, though, the boat **listed** to one side. **Crates** of food **supplies tumbled** into the waves.

"Everyone to shore!" Yuka shouted from the helm. "We've **run aground!**"

RUN AGROUND!

JOEL AND NINA and Mrs. Popper **crouched** at the edge of the **tilt**ing boat, staring into the **turbulent** gray-black water between them and the icy shore. Even though they had **huddled** together, they were **shivering**. The Arctic wind cut between the **fibers** of their coats and **rip**ped the heat away from their bodies. The **prospect** of being wet on top of being so cold was not **appealing** at all.

"Now, kids, wait until I've gone across, then I'll help you," Mrs. Popper said. Her words were brave, but she didn't look ready to cross the **slant**ing gangway[1] to the **slippery** rocks, not at all.

Mae, **nestled** in Nina's **mittens**, took one look up at her . . . and then **leaped** right into the sea!

"Mae, no!" Nina called. But Mae **transform**ed once she hit the water, turning from **awkward** puffball[2] to **sleek** missile. She **arrow**ed through the surf, then sprang out with such force that she landed a few yards[3] onto the rocky land, rolling and rolling before she got to her feet.

Ernest joined her, arrowing through the water just as **capably**—only he **unfortunately** landed in the very same **spot** as Mae, **bowl**ing her **over** and sending them both **tumbling** across the ground, **squawk**ing all the while. They got to their feet and stared at their human **companion**s **expectant**ly. *Come on, this is fun!*

"I think **the tables** are **turn**ing," Joel said. "The moment we cross over this water, *they're* the ones who are in their **element**, and we're the outsiders."

---

1 gangway 배의 건널판. 배와 부두 사이에 다리처럼 걸쳐 놓은 판자를 말한다.
2 puffball 민들레 등의 꽃받침이 변해서 씨방의 맨 끝에 붙은 솜털 같은 것. 여기에서는 새끼 펭귄의 솜털이 보송보송한 모습을 비유적으로 나타낸 표현이다.
3 yard 길이의 단위 야드. 1야드는 약 0.91미터이다.

Mrs. Popper went first, just managing to keep her footing and **make it** to the island, **stagger**ing in her heavy fur-lined boots. Nina was next, using her mother's **outstretch**ed arm to **steady** herself. Finally came Joel, helped by both his sister and mother.

"We did it, Yuka!" Mrs. Popper called back toward the boat.

Yuka looked up from the engine, pulling a metal mask back from his face. His **weld**ing tool continued to **spark** as he cheered and waved. "That's great! The **caretaker's hut** is on the far side of the island. I'll come join you as soon as I know there's no more water coming in."

"Are you sure you don't want to come now?" Joel called. He would miss having Yuka nearby, the **zany** stories he told and his cheerful **outlook** on life and all his knowledge of **gizmos** and **gadgets**. Life felt safer when he was around.

"We definitely don't want to **anchor** a **leak**ing boat, or we'll have an even bigger **crisis on our hands**," Yuka said. "I want to get us all back home before your break's over and my paper's due!"

"He's very **dedicated**, isn't he?" Mrs. Popper said. "The Popper Foundation put us in good hands."

"We'll come report back on what we discover!" Nina called, **skip**ping ahead across the rocks.

Joel shivered and **rub**bed his arms. "Let's go find

that hut."

"Maybe there are s'mores[4] there!" Nina called over her shoulder.

Mrs. Popper **nibble**d on the thumb of her mitten, a sure sign she was worried. "I don't think there are going to be any s'mores there, sweetie. Don't get your hopes up."

Joel gave her arm a rub. "Don't worry, Mom. This is going to be okay."

"I should be **comfort**ing *you*," she said.

"And we should be comforting *them*," Joel said. "But that's not how it's working out." He pointed ahead, where Mae and Ernest were waddling their way along the **barren** ground, getting right back up each time they fell down—which was often—on the island's icy rocks.

Nina led the **charge**, **scrambling** to **catch up** to the little penguin **chick**s. The Poppers were **out of breath** by the time they reached them. Together the group **crest**ed a rise so they could **take in** the whole of the island.

It was rocky and treeless, a mountaintop surrounded by **frigid** seas. **Boulder**s rose in strange **formation**s, making much of the island **impassable**. The sides of all the stones were **streak**ed in white—maybe penguin **poo**,

---

4 s'more 스모어. 두 개의 통밀 비스킷 사이에 초콜릿과 불에 구운 마시멜로(marshmallow)
를 끼워서 먹는 디저트.

maybe from other seabirds.

"Where *are* the Popper Penguins?" Joel asked.

"The hut is on the north of the island, on the other side of those big boulders," Mrs. Popper said. "It's next to the beach, where boats are *supposed* to land if they don't want to hit rocks and get big holes **gash**ed into them."

"A beach!" Nina said, clapping her hands. "That sounds great."

"A very cold beach," Joel added **soberly**. He knew his sister's mind had probably gone right to sunblock[5] and sandcastles.

They picked their way along the rocks. Joel tried to carry Ernest as they went, but the penguin made an *oork* of **outrage** and **nip**ped Joel's finger. **Apparent**ly the chicks preferred to travel on their own two feet now that they were in their sort of environment.

As the Poppers **made their way** around a final sharp **outcropping** of rock, the caretaker's hut came into view.

It was a **teeter**ing brown **shack**, its **planks warp**ed and darkened by sea air. A few of its **shingles** were loose, **clap**ping against the frame.

"It doesn't seem like anyone is home," Joel said.

---

5   **sunblock** 선블록 또는 자외선 차단제. 자외선으로부터 피부를 보호하고 햇볕에 그을리는 것을 방지하기 위해 바르는 크림.

"No, it definitely doesn't appear that way," Mrs. Popper said.

"Would you look at that?" Joel said, pointing above the front door as they approached.

"What? I can't see!" Nina said, jumping up and down. Mrs. Popper picked Nina up and held her high enough so she could read. Nina took her time, sounding out the words. "Here marks the hut built by Mr. Popper and Admiral Drake, the two gentlemen who brought penguins to the Arctic. Nineteen hundred and thirty-six."

"Mr. Popper was actually *here*!" Joel said. "That's so cool."

Once they'd made their way inside, they found a cabinet with cans of food, a gas stove, a simple sort of ship's radio, and a sleeping **platform** with woolen blankets.

"Those men weren't into luxuries, were they?" Mrs. Popper said.

"They were *explorers*," Nina said **indignantly**. "Of course they weren't into luxuries."

"It does seem like they could at least have put in a reading lamp," Mrs. Popper said.

"Let's get this place heated up," Joel said as he worked on **latch**ing the door closed.

"Look, a piece of paper," Nina said, after **rummaging** around under the bed. "Something's written on it!"

"Read it out loud," Mrs. Popper said as she did an **inventory** of the canned foods.

"You can do it this time," Nina said, **thrust**ing the paper at her brother.

Joel **cleared his throat**. "'To whomever it may **concern**: Please forgive my leaving my **post**. I developed a toothache that's making it impossible to **monitor** the Popper Penguins for the time being. I will return as soon as it's fixed and I've had a chance to see my family.'"

"**That's it?**" Nina asked.

"Yep," Joel said, after turning the paper over to check.

"When is it dated?" Mrs. Popper asked.

"Um . . . a month ago."

"Is that long enough for . . ." Mrs. Popper let her words **trail off.**

"Long enough for what?" Joel asked.

"It's just that . . . that there's no sign of the Popper Penguins. Could something have happened to them after the caretaker left?"

"Oh no!" Nina said, **clutch**ing Mae close to her.

"Oh no, indeed." Mrs. Popper **sigh**ed as she looked through the cabinets. "Aside from the state of the Popper Penguins, we have something else to worry about. There's only about three days' worth of food here."

"But Yuka needs more time than that to repair the boat," Joel said.

"Wait, what does that mean?" Nina asked.

Joel shook his head and **buried** his face in Ernest's soft side. "It means we're in big trouble."

Which was **precisely** when they heard a **chorus** of *orks* from the beach outside the hut.

Chapter 12

THE POPPER PENGUINS

THERE WERE PENGUINS outside the caretaker's hut.
Many, many penguins. They milled about, staring at
the hut and swaying back and forth, making a raucous
chorus of *orks* and *jooks* and *gaws*. One by one they
stepped forward, turned in a circle, then returned to the
group. It looked like some kind of welcome dance.

"Are those . . . the Popper Penguins?" Nina asked.

"I think so," Joel said. "You remember the penguin

statues in Stillwater? These look just like them. They have the same white lines on their cheeks that the Popper Penguins had, too."

"There's a lot more than twelve of these, though!" Mrs. Popper exclaimed.

Penguins kept arriving. They emerged from the surf, springing onto land just like Mae and Ernest had. They were confident as they sped through the water but became nervous and hesitant as soon as they were on the shore, scanning around to see what their friends were doing before they committed to walking up onto the beach. There they each did their turnabout dance

before huddling into the group, **craning** around one another to get the best view of the hut and the people emerging from it.

"Hello there," Mrs. Popper said, raising her hand in **greet**ing.

"*Ork! Ork! Ork!*" The penguins fell back in fear, one **bump**ing into the next until they all **pitch**ed over like a set of bowling pins, rolling and **scatter**ing into the ocean.

"We're sorry!" Nina called, hands cupped around her mouth. "We didn't mean to scare you. Please come back!"

As if they'd understood her words, the birds reemerged, lining up again along the beach and watching them **alert**ly.

"This is a **relief**," Joel said. "I'm glad the penguins are okay."

Nina **kneel**ed, holding her arms out. "Hi, everyone."

The birds turned **skittish** again, pressing into one another, the front row fully turning their backs on the Poppers. All except one, who made a loud *jook* and **toddle**d forward. Once she had neared the family, she **tilt**ed her head to look at them **inquiring**ly.

"What do you think she wants?" Nina asked.

"She wants us to **feed** her a fish, I'm sure of it!" Mrs. Popper said.

The penguin shook her head **sharply**, then **raced** into the surf, getting down onto her **belly** to **slide** like a toboggan[1] until she'd disappeared underwater. She was gone under the surface for a minute, then emerged— with a fish in her mouth! She toddled up the beach until she was in front of Mrs. Popper, then dropped the **wriggling** fish onto the rock.

Mrs. Popper looked down at it.

"I think you're supposed to eat it," Joel **whisper**ed, **nudging** her.

"I am?" Mrs. Popper said through **gritt**ed teeth.

The penguin toddled forward, gave the wriggling fish a **peck**, and then looked up at Mrs. Popper **expectant**ly. The penguin had a **patch** of extra white color on her head. That became her name in Joel's mind: Patch.

Mrs. Popper **lean**ed down and managed to pick up the fish in her **mittens**. It stared at her with its big, **bulging** eyes, **gills flaring**.

She opened her mouth.

She closed her mouth.

Looking Patch in the eyes, to make sure she wasn't **offend**ing her, Mrs. Popper gave the fish a **friendly pat**.

---

1 toboggan 터보건. 바닥이 평평하고 긴 목제 썰매로, 앞이 위로 구부러지고 양옆에 손잡이가 달려 있으며 비탈진 눈 위나 얼음 위에서 탄다. 이 책에서는 '터보건을 타듯 미끄러져 내려가다'라는 뜻의 동사로도 사용되었다.

Apparently that was enough of an **acknowledgment** of the present. Patch gave a **triumphant squawk** and **waddle**d back to the others. They greeted her in a joyful chorus, as if she'd just gotten back from a long journey.

"**Negotiation** successful!" Joel said.

Once the penguins' attention was drawn away, Mrs. Popper **toss**ed the **startled** fish back into the ocean.

Nina looked disappointed. "We need that food!"

"Yes," Mrs. Popper said. "But I think we might want to cook our fish first."

"But you still didn't have to throw that one back!"

"Yes, I suppose that's true," Mrs. Popper said, **smooth**ing the front of her coat. "I got **fluster**ed because I didn't know what to do, what can I say."

Right at that moment, another fish landed at the Poppers' feet. In fact, Joel realized, it might be the very same fish that Patch had brought them earlier. She'd emerged from the surf while they were talking and stood proudly over the **retrieve**d fish.

"I think we'd better get a cooking fire started," Mrs. Popper said.

BLEAK PROSPECTS

THE POPPER PENGUINS would go right up to the **doorway** of the caretaker's hut, but they seemed unwilling to enter. They'd crowd in front of it, **goad**ing one another to go **investigate**, but none of them was willing to **take the plunge** and push open the door. Not even Patch was up to it, though she would **occasional**ly work up the courage to **spy** through the window.

"Maybe they're worried that we're secretly sea lions[1]

dressed up as humans and that we'll eat them right up," Joel said as he arranged his schoolbooks on the **lumpy** bed. His mother had informed him that, even in a survival situation, he'd have to **keep up** on his studies.

"It's **silly** for penguins to be afraid of us," Nina said. "At least Mae and Ernest aren't, are you?"

What Mae and Ernest were afraid of was the other penguins! The chicks hid behind the curtain covering the hut's window, occasionally **peeking** out at the big adult penguins, then hiding back away. Always the more nervous of the two, Ernest had taken to **diving** under Mae for protection. Of course, only his head fit, so the rest of him **splay**ed out on the **windowsill**.

"We aren't exactly raising the most **courageous** chicks the world has ever known, are we?" Mrs. Popper observed.

"It's only because they've led such **shelter**ed lives so far," Nina said. "I think they'll find their place in the world once they've had time to **adjust**."

"I don't know, they seem to have a long way to go," Joel said. He **sidled** over to the hut's propane[2] **stove**, its sole source of warmth. His mother was cooking a pair of fish

---

1 sea lion 바다사자. 물갯과의 바다짐승. 몸의 길이는 3미터, 몸무게는 500~1100kg 정도로 바다사자류 가운데 가장 크며, 옅은 적갈색이고 털은 없다. 주둥이가 넓고 머리가 크고 목이 굵은 것이 특징이다.

2 propane 프로판. 무색무취의 가연성 기체로 상온에서 압력을 가하면 쉽게 액화한다. 액화 석유 가스의 주성분을 이루며 가정용이나 자동차 등의 연료가 된다.

on a pan. A third fish had been left **raw** and cut up on a tin plate, where it was serving as the chicks' meal. "When's our dinner ready?"

"In a few minutes," Mrs. Popper said. "Then I'll cook up a couple more fish to bring to Yuka."

"Well, we're **definitely** not going to **run out** of fish anytime soon," Nina said, pointing to the beach outside the window, where a **neat pile** of fish had **accumulat**ed. Whenever one of the penguins went on a fishing **excursion**, it would return with an extra fish to leave at the Poppers' door.

"I wonder if this is a **trick** Mr. Popper taught them years ago," Joel said.

"Our biggest danger won't be running out of food, but running out of **fuel**," Mrs. Popper said. "If that happens, we'll be very, very cold."

"How much is left?"

She **rap**ped her **knuckle**s against the side of the can. It rang out **hollow**ly. "I'm not sure. I hope enough for a few days."

"You *hope*?" Nina said, her lower lip suddenly **wobbling**.

"Don't worry, darling," Mrs. Popper said. "The boat will be fixed by then. Or at least Yuka will have power **restore**d so we can live on the boat until it's ready to make the return journey."

Joel **kneel**ed down to **stroke** Mae's **fuzzy** back. "Maybe by then our chicks will be brave enough to introduce themselves to the other penguins."

"They're trying to find new parents," Nina said. "That can't be easy!"

"Yeah," Joel said, settling both chicks into his **lap** and **pet**ting them. "Don't let us **rush** you two."

Soon after Mrs. Popper was back from bringing Yuka his cooked fish, nighttime dropped quick and dark. Still in their coats, the Popper family closed the hut's door, huddling together on the mattress with its **scratchy** but warm woolen blanket. The chicks **tuck**ed themselves under it.

The wind **howl**ed, each **gust** making the walls of the hut **shudder**. As he **drift**ed toward sleep, Joel imagined a sea beast was **hurl**ing its **tentacle**s against the hut. Popper Island was fun by day, but at night it was a strange and scary place. He was glad that they were all together, that he had Nina and his mother near. He hoped Yuka was okay.

Mae and Ernest **burrow**ed closer as the wind got louder. Joel was glad that he had them alongside him, too.

The next morning, Nina was the first to wake. The air in the hut was so cold that it was hard to feel the **tip** of her nose. But under the wool blanket it was nice and warm. The wind had died down, and instead was . . . what *was* that sound?

Penguin chick **snore**s! Nina held her ear against Ernest's **beak** and listened to the soft **wheezy** sound. Maybe he was dreaming—she could see his eyes moving **rapid**ly beneath his **lid**s.

Mrs. Popper **sigh**ed and got out of bed, opening the propane valve so she could light the stove. "You kids stay in bed until the hut's warmed up, okay?"

But Nina couldn't wait that long. She **crept** to the hut's door and eased it open.

The sunlight was bright over the thin **layer** of **crackly** ice that had formed on the **pebble**s of the beach. The

Popper Penguins were already hard at work, toddling all over the shore, fishing and eating and carrying on. They would **toss** their heads back as they made loud calls to one another, **exposing** their beautiful long necks.

Joel joined Nina at the doorway, the chicks in his arms. He gently **lean**ed down and **release**d them onto the cold ground. They looked around, **panic**ked, and then tried to **retreat** into the hut—until Nina closed the door behind them. They *oork*ed in **protest**.

"This is for your own good," Joel explained. "You have to get used to other penguins!"

The chicks looked out at the cold sea. It wasn't hard to imagine what they were thinking: Wouldn't it be so much nicer to stay in bed?

Patch tobogganed over and stood, toddling toward the **frighten**ed chicks. "*Jook!*" she said with a toss of her beak.

Ernest dived under Mae. Mae, though, looked bravely up at the strange penguin. Then she made her first adult penguin noise. "*Ork!*"

Patch **clack**ed her beak against Mae's a few times. Clearly feeling **embolden**ed, Ernest emerged and held his beak out, his eyes widening in **delight** when Patch clacked his, too.

Then the penguin walked along the beach, looking over her shoulder. The message was clear: *Come with me!*

That's just what Ernest and Mae did. After looking up at Nina and Joel for **approval**, they toddled after Patch.

"I think we'd better go along!" Joel said as the three penguins made their way along the beach.

"Mom, we're **exploring** with Mae and Ernest!" Nina called out. "We won't go far."

"Be very careful!" Mrs. Popper said. Another mother might not have let her children **wander** an **Arctic** island on their own. But Mrs. Popper knew that her kids would be careful.

"We'll be back by breakfast!" Joel called as he and his sister scrambled along the beach after their chicks and their new friend, rocks **crunch**ing under their feet.

"A penguin wants to show us something!" Nina **huff**ed as she jogged along the beach, ice breaking and **tinkling** under her boots. "How exciting!"

SHOW AND TELL[1]

AS THEY HIKED along the **frozen** beach, more and more of the Popper Penguins emerged from the surf to join them. Each time a new penguin neared, the **chicks** would go **motionless**, making their baby-like *oork* sounds, until they **summon**ed enough courage to **let out** an adult *ork*.

---

1 show and tell 유치원이나 초등학교에서 각자 자신에게 의미 있는 물건을 가지고 나와서 친구들과 선생님에게 설명하는 일종의 발표 시간.

The process would repeat itself each time a new Popper Penguin joined the **procession.**

For such **sleek** creatures, the penguins were **ungainly** on the shore. They **tipped over** this way and that the moment they hit a **slippery patch**, more often than not **knock**ing over another bird in the process. Joel and Nina kept near the chicks, so they wouldn't **inadvertent**ly get **squish**ed by a rolling stranger.

Patch led them up a bank of rocks between the rough surfaces with her **flexible** feet. Many of the other penguins tried to make the jumps but **gave up** after a few **dramatic** falls. They made *orks* of **outrage** as they **retreat**ed into the surf.

Mae **courageous**ly tried to make the first **leap,** but **bonk**ed her head on a **protruding** rock. She **glared** at it **stern**ly. *"Gaw!"*

"Seems like you still need us," Nina said as she and Joel each picked up a chick and **clamber**ed up the rocks.

They drew their coats and scarves tighter as they crossed a **windswept plateau.** The ocean wind carried **spray**s of ice that **stung** their cheeks and noses. When they **released** the chicks to the ground, the birds **seized up,** holding their little wings tight to their bodies and **scrunch**ing their eyes closed. Joel and Nina each **tuck**ed a chick into their warm coats.

All the while, Patch led them along.

Popper Island wasn't large. Before twenty minutes had gone by, they were at the center. There, the penguin made a sharp turn, then brought them to the eastern **edge**.

Patch reached a **precipice** and turned around, making a loud *ork* as she **gestured** with one **flipper**.

Nina and Joel went to join her and saw that here the ground turned into a sharp **cliff**. **Nest**ing down the **vertical** rocky surface were birds that looked a lot like penguins. They had the same white-and-black coloration,[2]

---

2   coloration 천연색(天然色). 만물이 자연 그대로 갖추고 있는 빛깔.

only they were smaller and had clown-like faces that ended in bright red **bill**s. Joel felt like they looked like **inferior** penguins. Then one **spread** its wings and **swoop**ed over the sea far below. They could fly. That was **definite**ly a point in their favor.

"I think those are puffins!³" Nina said. "Neat. I've always wanted to see a puffin."

The kids released Mae and Ernest so the chicks could see the puffins, too. It was clearly still too cold for them— they stuck to the warm **nook**s between the kids' legs. They did look out curiously, though, making startled little **gasp**s whenever a puffin took flight. "I hope we're not making them jealous," Nina said, "not being able to fly and all."

Joel **notice**d that Patch kept pointing at the puffins with her wing. She wanted them to notice something.

He looked more closely. The puffins all seemed quite skinny. Some had **tuft**s of hair sticking out in random places. They didn't look sleek like the island's penguins.

"I see egg**shell**s around, but no chicks," Nina said. "That's **odd**, right?"

"And look!" Joel said. "The puffins will make short flights over the water, but they never return with any fish."

---

3 puffin 퍼핀 또는 코뿔바다오리. 시베리아와 알래스카 부근의 바다와 해안 절벽 등에 서식하며, 등쪽은 검은색이고 얼굴 측면, 가슴과 배는 흰색이다. 검은색과 흰색의 대비가 뚜렷하며, 크고 화려한 색의 부리가 특징이다.

Mae and then Ernest toddled over to Patch, taking **shelter** beneath her **belly**. The penguin **patient**ly accepted the chicks while she continued to point at the puffins. She made sad *ork*s, opening and closing her beak.

"I think I get it," Nina said, looking at the penguins and then the suffering puffin **colony**.

"What is it?" Joel asked.

"The puffins were the only birds around before. So they were the only ones eating the **local** fish. But now there are all these penguins here."

". . . and the penguins are eating all the good fish," Joel said, "which means there's not enough food left for the puffins."

Patch made a **satisfied**-sounding *ork*. These **dense** humans had finally **figure**d **out** what was going on.

A GATHERING STORM

WHEN THE CHILDREN returned to the **caretaker's hut**, they found Yuka and their mother standing outside. They looked like adults often do when they're worried—very still, arms crossed, **staring** hard. Joel and Nina sped up, in case they were the reason the grown-ups were anxious. But their mother kept her arms crossed even after she'd seen them.

"Oh, good, you're back," she said.

"What's going on?" Joel asked, **shading** his eyes against the low sun, trying to see what had captured all of his mother's attention.

Yuka shook his head and put on a tight smile. "Nothing you need to **concern** yourselves about."

"There's no point hiding it from them," Mrs. Popper said. "Kids deserve to know the truth."

"*What* truth?" Nina asked, her face turning red.

"The boat is nearly fixed," Yuka said, his face lighting up.

"Oh," Joel said, **confus**ed. "That's *good* news, right?"

"Yes," he said. "I just wanted to start with some of that. Ahem. The bad news is that, well, you can see for

yourself." Yuka pointed to the southern sky, where a bank of dark clouds had formed.

"That *does* look like bad news," Nina said, **nod**ding.

"It's coming our way," Mrs. Popper explained, "and an Arctic storm is serious business. We can't sail out until it's passed over."

"And we don't know when it will end," Yuka said. "If my **instrument**s had been working correctly, we'd have known about it on our way here and could have headed to the **mainland** earlier."

A **mournful** *oork* came from within Joel's coat. "I think Ernest is very sorry about the **sabotage**," Joel said.

"Yuka will be staying with us in the hut while the storm is **raging**," Mrs. Popper said.

"We've got a few hours left," he said. "Your mother wants to stay here to get the hut ready, but would you two come with me to the boat? We need to **retrieve** whatever **supplies** we can before the wind and snow come. There will be no crossing the island later."

Nina and Joel nodded **somberly**. "Of course."

Together they hiked across the island to the boat and returned with as many supplies as they could carry— which was not, truth be told, all that many. A lot of them had been lost **overboard** during the **wreck**.

When they returned to the caretaker's hut, Yuka and

Joel and Nina each had a **crate** in their arms. They piled them in a corner of the room. Ernest and Mae **hop**ped down from the **windowsill**, where they had been **keep**ing **tabs on** the Popper Penguins. They **huddle**d into the **comfort** of the kids' **ankles**.

The wind outside began to **howl.** Yuka looked out the window at the sky, his expression turning **grim**. "Maybe there's less time than I thought. There might be long enough for only one more trip to the boat."

"I'm ready," Nina said.

"No, you two stay here," Yuka said. "I don't want to risk your being **trap**ped outside when the winds start."

They watched from the window as Yuka headed back to his boat. Once he'd disappeared from view, Mrs. Popper clapped her hands **brisk**ly. "Let's get everything put away, so the hut's in the best order we can get it. We might be **stuck** inside for a long time."

Ernest and Mae watched **grave**ly as the Poppers prepared the hut. Joel shook out the **spare coverlet** and **drape**d it over a **makeshift** bed of pillows on the floor, so Yuka would have somewhere to sleep. Nina and Mrs. Popper lined up the food supplies. "Lots of canned beans!" Nina **announce**d.

"And some tuna fish, I hope?" Joel asked, **pat**ting Ernest on the head.

"Of course," Nina said. "Though I think *we're* going to

eat that, now that the penguins have been delivering **raw fish**."

"Oh no, the Popper Penguins!" Joel said, **peer**ing out the hut's small window. "Do you think they're going to be okay, Mom?"

She **squeeze**d Joel's shoulder. "Of course they'll be okay. They've survived many winters out here. They're designed for this sort of weather. It's primates[1] like us who have to worry."

When Yuka reappeared at the doorway, he had **icicle**s hanging from his hood, and the **stubble** on his **chin glitter**ed with **frost**. The wind **roar**ed into the hut, **scatter**ing the pillows Joel had carefully arranged and knocking over a tower of canned beans. Yuka **slam**med the door closed and **stamp**ed his booted feet. "Wow. I guess I went through storms like this in my childhood, but this seems worse than any of those ever were."

"Were you able to radio the **authorities** while you were at the boat?" Mrs. Popper asked.

Yuka shook his head. "No, sorry. The electrical systems aren't up yet. But we're going to be fine. And the Popper **Foundation** knows our **itinerary**, so if we're missing for long enough, they'll be sure to send help."

---

1 primate 영장류. 가장 고등하며 물건을 잡을 수 있는 손과 발이 있는 척추동물을 통틀어 이르는 말. 손발톱이 달린 다섯 개의 손가락과 발가락이 있고, 직립할 수 있다.

The walls **shudder**ed. Ernest made an *oork* of **panic** and hopped onto the bed.

"I think Ernest has the right idea," Joel said, **zip**ping his coat up tight before following the penguin chick under the covers.

Chapter 16

STRANGE BEDFELLOWS

THE NEXT TWO days passed in a **blur**. Once the storm clouds covered the **Arctic** sun, there was little outside light coming into the hut, so it was hard to know whether it was day or night. It didn't much matter, anyway—there was no going outside, whatever time it was. All Nina knew was that the **tempest** shook the roof and set the walls **trembling**, that it snaked cold fingers under the door and through the double-**paned** glass of the window, that the only **defense** was to huddle under the **comforter**, hoping the storm didn't decide to take the roof off entirely.

By drawing her hood **string**s tight, Nina was able to have only her nose **expose**d. But even so, she could feel her body growing colder. Though she knew it would make her arm **tingle** from the cold air, she reached out to touch the heater. It felt like ice.

Nina **tuck**ed her arm back under the covers. "Mom," she said softly, "I think the propane **ran out**."

"Oh no," Mrs. Popper said. She reached out, touched the **stove**, and **gasp**ed. "You're right. Huddle down, children. Are you okay, Yuka?"

"Yes," he said from his **pile** of pillows. But he couldn't keep the **shiver**s out of his voice.

The winds continued to howl, and the temperature continued to drop. Joel and Nina drew close to their mother, **snuggling** in as near as they could—even though under any other **circumstance**s, Joel would have claimed he was too old for such a thing.

"Don't worry, kids," Mrs. Popper said. Nina knew her mother only said that when she *was* worried, of course.

"I'm not afraid!" Nina said.

"Me neither!" Joel said. Nina could almost believe him.

Despite their worry, they all grew sleepy, and gradually Nina sensed her thoughts growing **scatter**ed. Then she must have fallen asleep, because she became **aware** of waking up. The wind was howling louder than ever, and as she fully opened her eyes, she realized why.

Someone had opened the door.

"Mom!" Nina said **urgently**. But her mother kept **snoring**.

Long shadows grew across the floor as the **intruder**—no, intruder*s*—came in closer.

Their shadows were shaped sort of like bowling pins.

It was the Popper Penguins. At least two **dozen** Popper Penguins.

The birds were lined up in the **doorway**, facing in. Mae and Ernest must have sensed their kind nearby.

They rolled onto the ground from under the comforter and were facing the adult penguins, making nervous *oork* sounds.

Nina **nudge**d her brother. "Joel. *Penguins!* In the hut!"

He **grunt**ed and rolled over in his sleep, pulling the wool blanket over his head.

The Popper Penguins **waddle**d forward, **cautious**ly **investigating** the hut, taking careful **peck**s of the cabinets, the walls, the boots lined up by the doorway. Once the first ones had freed up space in the opening, more **file**d in from behind. Nina wouldn't have thought penguins ever could look cold, but these ones certainly did. They had **frost** on their feathered **eyebrow**s, along their **beak**s, on the **tip**s of their dark, dinosaur-like feet.

Nina nudged Joel again. "*More* penguins!"

Soon they'd filled the entire floor of the hut, their *ork*s and *jook*s filling the air, while the wind from the storm outside **whistle**d.

Once the last of the Popper Penguins was inside the **shelter** of the hut, Patch pressed her flipper against the door and pushed it closed.

Even though Joel had managed to sleep through the **clamor** of a roomful of penguins, *that* sound was what woke him up. "Wow" was all he could think to say.

Yuka sat up amid his pillows. "I guess they must be

cold, too."

Surprised by Yuka's deep voice, the penguins **panic**ked, **tumbling** over one another, **bump**ing into the walls and cabinets before **heap**ing into a great **squawk**ing pile. Once the two dozen penguins had righted themselves, Yuka was **trapped**, sitting **bolt upright** in the center of them. His eyebrows disappeared right into his hairline, he was that surprised.

"Kids," he said, "I'm **stuck** in a waddle of penguins!"

"Do you need help?" Nina asked, **tugg**ing on her **furry** slippers.

Yuka considered the question for a moment. "No, actually," he said, appearing to surprise even himself. "This is may be the **coziest** I've been in my whole life. Turns out penguins are excellent **insulators**!"

Before anyone could stop her, Nina had **scrambled** out of bed and into the midst of the birds. They made their panicked noises again but didn't **bowl** one another **over** this time. They were more comfortable with Nina.

"Oh, wow," Nina said. "He's right. This is **amazing!**"

Joel joined her in the huddle of penguins. Their feathery coats were **smooth** and warm and smelled of fish and seawater. "Whoa. It's really nice."

Just then their mother woke up. "Kids, where are you?" she asked as she cleared the sleep from her eyes. Her

jaw dropped wide open once she saw her children and Yuka, waving at her from the huddle of penguins.

"You have to try this, Mom!" Nina said.

THE HUDDLE

CROWDING IN WITH penguins turned out to be a wonderful way to **ride out** a storm. The birds were amazingly warm and soft. But it was more than that. Even though **fearsome** things were happening, even after the propane **ran out** and Arctic night fell and the wind **howl**ed louder and louder, the penguins kept up a **stream** of **chatter**. It was a great **distract**ion—it was harder to stay scared when there was so much to **eavesdrop** on.

"I think this tall one next to me doesn't like the short one next to you," Nina said to Joel. "He keeps throwing his head back and making a lot of noise in the short one's direction."

"I think that's because he *does* like him," Joel said. "This short one is the warmest of them all."

"What are you kids talking about?" Mrs. Popper called out. She was pinned between penguins, just like the rest of them, only she was **stuck** on the far side of the hut.

"The puffins are **starving!**" Nina said, but her voice was lost in the **ruckus** of penguin cries.

"What did you say?" Mrs. Popper shouted.

"We'll tell you later!" Nina said.

"WHAT?"

"WE'LL TELL YOU—never mind," Nina said, letting her voice get lost in the bird **chorus**.

Come **dawn**, the winds died down and the penguins filed out of the hut one by one, each taking a moment to wave goodbye before heading off to fish. "I'm getting the sense that this isn't the first time the penguins have ridden out the worst of a storm by keeping warm in the hut," Joel said, **stretch**ing his arms and legs to get the blood **circulating** again.

"I'm sure they're able to **tolerate** the most extreme cold, but I can't blame them for taking a better option when it becomes available! No wonder the caretaker needed a break," Mrs. Popper said. "I'm not sure how much more I could take of that."

"I thought it was fantastic," Nina said. "And they have good skills with door handles!"

"Yeah, I kind of miss them already," Joel added. He **swoop**ed down to pick up Ernest and Mae, who were looking around with **astonish**ed expressions on their faces, as if **debating** whether the flood of adult penguins had been a dream.

He was answered by a *plop, plop, plop* from the open doorway. Joel peered out. During the storm the rocks of Popper Island had disappeared under a **layer** of white snow and ice, **sparkling** in the morning sun. On top of that ice lay three fish.

Before Joel's eyes, Patch **emerged** from the surf, waddled over, and **regurgitated** a fish onto the ice. It was a **terrific** production, with lots of **hack**ing and **heaving** and **shrieking**. The fish was **slick** with **stomach fluids**.

"Ew," Joel said, even as Ernest and Mae hopped down from his arms, **toddle**d over, and **scarf**ed down the fish with *orks* of joy.

"That's good," Nina said, pulling her hat low over her ears as she joined Joel in the doorway. "I'm glad Ernest and Mae took care of that, because I don't think I was up for eating **barf** fish."

"Yes," Joel replied. "I'm with you."

Yuka **slip**ped out of the hut and walked right past the penguin-**puke**d fish, un**impress**ed. The **spiky** crampons[1] on his boots **crunch**ed through the fresh ice as he headed to the boat. "Back to work! I'm hoping to be finished with the repair by the end of the day."

"Thank you, Yuka!" Mrs. Popper called from within the hut.

Joel looked at Ernest, who had just finished **gobbling** down his second fish. Ernest looked up at Joel proudly, **flutter**ing his **fuzzy** wings.

"Ernest and Mae haven't made any penguin friends yet," Nina said.

"I'm worried about them, too," Joel said. "There's only a few hours left, and we don't know if they'll be okay after we leave."

---

1 crampon 크램폰 또는 아이젠. 여러 개의 뾰족한 못이 박혀 있는 모양으로 경사가 심한 빙벽이나 단단한 설사면 등을 오르내릴 때, 미끄러짐을 방지하기 위해 등산화 밑창에 부착하는 장비.

A NEW DESTINATION

JOEL AND NINA and Mrs. Popper lined up on the shoreline, looking at the **rock**ing boat. **Beat**en metal covered the hole the Popper Island **shoals** had made in the **hull**. Yuka had **neat**ly **weld**ed it on with **strips** of light gray solder.[1] "Looks pretty good, right?" Yuka said, **rap**ping his **knuckles** on the hull. It rang out brightly.

---

1   solder 땜납. 불에 잘 녹고 쇠붙이에 잘 붙는 성질을 지니고 있어서, 금이 가거나 뚫어진 쇠붙이를 때울 때 사용하는 녹는점이 낮은 합금.

"It does. Great work!" Mrs. Popper said.

Joel tried to add his voice, but **the pit in his stomach** was making it hard even to speak. Ernest was tight in his arms, **snoring** away.

How was Joel going to say what he needed to say?

Nina looked up at him. Normally she was the more **assertive** one, but **apparent**ly it was his turn this time around.

"Are you two okay?" Mrs. Popper asked.

"Yeah," Joel said, **nod**ding. Then he shook his head. "No. I mean, no."

"Yes, right, no," Nina said, nodding her head **energetic**ally and then shaking it just as energetically.

"You're both acting very **peculiar**."

"No **kid**ding," Yuka said, **narrow**ing his eyes. "I know none of us slept too well the last few nights, but you're being really **weird**."

"Okay, here goes," Joel said, taking his mom's hand and looking into her eyes so she would know to listen hard to him. "One of the penguins took us to the other side of the island, and there are puffins there, which should be great, but they're not healthy, not at all, they're all **scrawny** and their eggs are broken but there aren't any **chick**s, and the penguins are all fat and healthy, and we think that the problem is the penguins are eating all the fish around here and there's none left for the puffins, and they were here *first*, so that doesn't seem fair, does it?"

Mrs. Popper **stare**d at him, her mouth wide open. Then she finally put together his **stream** of words. She nodded. "So what do you want us to do?"

Nina coughed and stepped forward, maybe a little **dramatic**ally. "It might have been a good idea in the olden days for Mr. Popper to bring his penguins up here, but he didn't realize that it would make it hard for the puffins to survive, even all these **generation**s later. What if . . . what if we brought them to where they belong?"

"You mean, to the *Antarctic*?" Mrs. Popper said, hand over her chest.

"That's, um, very far from here," Yuka added.

"Yes," Nina said, tears entering her voice. "But then the penguins would all be in their proper home, with other penguins. And during the **voyage** Mae and Ernest would have more of a chance to **bond** with the rest of the group and find penguins to be their parents."

Mrs. Popper looked at Yuka. His face was completely still. Then, finally, he gave a little **shrug**. "If you all help me **pilot**, I could write my paper and send it to my professor along the way."

"And we have the winter break not so far off," Nina said quickly. "We'd only miss a couple extra weeks of school. In the meantime, we can work ahead in our textbooks."

"It would be *so* educational for us to go to **Antarctica**, don't you think?" Joel said.

"Yes, Mom, it's an opportunity not to be missed," Nina said, nodding eagerly.

Mrs. Popper looked at her children, then at the **dozing** Mae and Ernest, tight in their arms. "I suppose we could see if it's possible."

Nina jumped up and down, then remembered Mae and stopped. The penguin chick didn't wake, though— she must not have slept in the **ruckus** last night, either. She gave a soft, fish-**scent**ed **burp** while she slept.

"But, kids," Mrs. Popper said, "just how do you **propose** we get two **dozen** wild penguins to board a boat?"

Joel **paused**. They'd been so busy worrying about how to **convince** Mom that they hadn't considered *this* problem.

Yuka coughed. "The **ancestor**s of these penguins arrived here on a boat, so maybe it won't be so very unfamiliar to them."

"You mean the penguins might have been **pass**ing **down** stories about their trip here?" Mrs. Popper asked, **eyebrow**s raised.

"Stranger things have happened," Yuka said, shrugging.

Nina **tugg**ed on her mom's **sleeve**. "Mom, *Mom*! If

that's true, maybe they've been passing down other stories about the original Popper Penguins. Remember, they used to have a *circus act*, where they ***marched in formation*?"

Joel realized where his sister was going, and clapped. That woke Ernest up, who gave an **outraged grunt** and rolled over to fall back asleep in Joel's arms.

Chapter
19

THE POPPER PENGUINS
PERFORM AN ENCORE

BACK IN THE 1930s, Popper's Performing Penguins had
paraded onstage to the "Merry Widow Waltz"[1] on the
piano. That was all well and good if you were getting
penguins to march in a music hall, but there were no
pianos on Popper Island.

---

1 Merry Widow Waltz 헝가리의 작곡가 프란츠 레하르(Franz Lehar)의 오페레타 '메리 위
도우(The Merry Widow)'에 나오는 음악.

The modern-day Poppers **made do**, though, by standing outside the **caretaker's hut** and **bang**ing on camping pots with spoons. They tried to be as rhythmic and musical as possible, but Joel and Nina kept losing each other's beats, so it was really more of a ruckus than a song. Still, the penguins lined up curiously on the beach, watching the noisemakers and adding *gork*s and *gaw*s of their own, making shy turns and pirouettes.[2]

When the Poppers began to **make their way** across the icy rocks from the beach to the boat, Nina almost

---

2 pirouette 피루엣. 발레에서 한쪽 발로 서서 빠르게 도는 춤 동작.

didn't **dare** look back to see if the penguins were behind them. But when she did, there was the line of penguins, following single **file**, adding their chorus of voices to the **glorious** noise.

"The **Arctic** will never see anything like this again," Yuka said. From the look on his face, he thought that was for the best.

When they reached the boat, the Poppers went right to the **bow** to make as much space as possible. There they all were: Mrs. Popper and Nina and Joel, still banging on camping pots, Mae and Ernest at their feet. The rest of the **deck** was **wall-to-wall** penguins, with Yuka at the **stern**, gently **nudging** away the nearby birds so he could start the boat's engine.

When the deck began to **rumble** under their feet, the penguins *ork*ed and **milled** about, **bump**ing into one another and **pecking** curiously at the floor. Mae and Ernest **imitate**d the big penguins, even though by now they knew perfectly well how the boat worked.

After taking up the **anchor**, Yuka **steer**ed away from Popper Island.

Joel and Nina stood at the stern, surrounded by their new penguin friends as they looked back at Popper Island. Two puffins were standing at their **cliff**, watching the **depar**ting boat. In **unison**, they each raised a wing.

"It's like they're saying goodbye," Joel said.

"Or maybe they're saying thank you," Nina said.

"Good luck, puffins!" Joel called, waving.

"Okay, children. Get working on your homework while there's still light out and the waves aren't too rough, please," Mrs. Popper called. "As soon as we're near enough to shore I'll call and get your updated **assignment**s."

"You'd think that when we're sailing through the Arctic with two dozen penguins, we could **skip** the normal school rules," Nina **grumble**d.

"Not when it's our mom," Joel said.

With that, they were off! The penguins were

fascinated by all aspects of the trip: the whitewater at the stern, the rumbling engines, the seabirds wheeling overhead. Much to Yuka's dismay, they were especially interested in the steering wheel, taking pecks at it as soon as his attention was distracted. Joel had to shoo Ernest away whenever he got renewed interest in investigating the boat's repaired computer.

Before Popper Island disappeared from view, they saw a puffin one more time, soaring over the water, swooping to catch a fish before heading back home.

GROWING PAINS

IT TOOK THEM six weeks to reach the **Antarctic**. By
that point Nina and Joel had gotten ahead on all their
schoolwork and were learning side topics: **avian** biology
for Joel and lines of latitude[1] for Nina. They'd stopped
in Hillport to **stock up** on fish, to get permission to

---

1 latitude 위도. 지구 위의 위치를 나타내는 좌표로, 적도를 중심으로 하여 남북(南北)으
   로 평행하게 그은 선이다. 적도로부터 남북으로 얼마나 떨어져 있는가에 대한 정도를 나
   타낸다.

temporarily withdraw the kids from school, and for Yuka to turn in his essay and pick up his research books so he could work on his **dissertation** during the **voyage**.

The Popper **Foundation** understood when the Poppers explained that the penguins had been **outcompeting** the native puffins in the Arctic. They gave Mrs. Popper and Yuka **stipend**s to **compensate** them for their work in **relocating** the penguins, and also paid for a **refrigeration** unit to be **install**ed belowdecks—the penguins would need to stay down there while the boat passed through the hot tropics.² (Two **sneak**ed out onto the deck anyway one night, and the kids found them there in the morning, overheating, **flipper**s **flung** out wide and mouths open. They never tried to sneak out again after that!)

By the time the boat had **round**ed the bottom of Argentina³ and was nearing the Antarctic, Mae and Ernest started to look . . . **odd**. "I think Mae is sick!" Nina said. She held up the penguin's wing so Joel could see her **torso** beneath, where a **patch** of gray **fluffy** feathers was missing.

---

2 tropics 열대. 적도를 중심으로 남북으로 각각 23도 27분을 지나는 위선(緯線) 사이에 있는 지대. 연평균 기온이 20℃ 이상 또는 최한월 평균 기온이 18℃ 이상인 지역으로, 연중 기온이 높고 강우량이 많은 것이 특징이다.

3 Argentina 아르헨티나. 남아메리카 남동부에 위치한 공화국으로, 농업, 공업, 그리고 축산업이 주된 산업이다 공용어는 에스파냐어이며, 수도는 부에노스아이레스(Buenos Aires)이다.

"She's not sick," Joel said, pointing to a picture in the avian biology textbook they'd checked out from the Hillport library. "She's **molt**ing. The same thing is happening to Ernest."

"It's normal?" Nina asked.

"Totally normal."

Over the final days of the voyage, Mae and Ernest would do their usual **preen**ing, **nip**ping at their feathers, only now big **clump**s of them would come away. Beneath were **reveal**ed **sleek** black feathers—their adult **plumage**! "Would you look at that," Nina said. "Our little penguins are growing up!"

"They look kind of like punk rockers,[4]" Joel said.

They might have started getting their adult feathers, but even over the six weeks of voyage, the chicks had yet to **bond** with the other penguins. While Joel was busy with his homework, Ernest would stand near the other birds, but the whole time he'd be looking over at Joel, as if asking whether he was allowed to come back yet. Mae was clearer about her feelings: She'd pick fights if any Popper Penguins came between her and Nina, only calming once she was back in her arms.

"They'll start **fitting in** eventually, right?" Nina asked Mrs. Popper.

"I'm sure," her mother replied. "Soon we'll be at the Drake Research Station, and we can ask the penguin experts there how we can help Mae and Ernest **adjust**. Now, it's getting **chillier**. Draw your scarves tight, children."

The very next day, Yuka called out and slowed the boat. The penguins all **gather**ed at the bow to see what had gotten his attention. Shore!

A **glacier** ran right up against the water, its surfaces going from white at the **edge**s to a **brilliant** blue in its **core**. At the far end of the giant **block** of ice was a **gravelly**

4　punk rock 펑크 록. 기존 록의 체제화에 반발하며 1970년대 중반 이후 영국의 런던과 미국의 뉴욕에서 시작된 연주 스타일. 단순하고 강렬한 코드와 빠른 리듬을 기반으로 과격하고 정열적인 사운드를 강조한다.

beach that rose up to a **stony bluff**. On top was a simple red building, with aluminum[5] sides and a **peak**ed, snow-covered roof.

"That's the Drake Center for Environmental Studies," Yuka said. "I've read a lot about it in my courses. They're doing important research about our **climate**. Who would have thought life would come to this—I grew up near the North **Pole**, but now I'm at the very other end of the planet!"

As they watched, a **figure emerge**d from the little red building and stood at the edge of the cliff. She waved at them as she brought a **megaphone** to her mouth. "Hello! I'm Dr. Antonia Drake. Welcome! You can bring your boat right up to the slip.[6]"

"Oh, good," Yuka said **under his breath**. "No shipwrecks this time."

By the time he had guided the boat to the **dock**, and Joel and Nina had **hop**ped to shore to tie it up tight, Dr. Drake had come down to **greet** them. "What a long journey you've had," she said. "You must be so tired."

"Not really!" Nina said. "We're mostly just excited."

"Who's that?" Dr. Drake asked, looking at the small

---

5 aluminum 알루미늄. 은백색의 가벼운 금속으로 가공하기 쉽고 가벼우며 내식성이 있다. 인체에 해가 없으므로 건축, 화학, 가정용 제품 등에 널리 쓴다.

6 slip 선대(船臺). 배를 만들 때에 선체를 올려놓고 작업하는 경사진 대를 말한다.

penguin by Nina's feet.

"That's Mae," Joel explained. "And this is Ernest. They look like adults now, but they just finished molting. They're the reason we started on this whole adventure!"

In fact, Ernest hadn't quite finished molting. He still had a **tuft** of fluffy feathers on the back of his head, like an old **bald**ing man.

"They need a little help learning to **socialize**—" Mrs. Popper said, then she had to stop and **concentrate** on not falling into the sea as twenty-four penguins marched along the boat and hopped past her onto the dock, nearly **knock**ing her over in the process.

Patch walked to the water's edge, **stared** in, then walked back. She **mustered** enough courage to return to the edge, then **lost her nerve** again and **waddled** back. Patch walked to the edge again, but this time another penguin crowded in behind her to see and **accidental**ly knocked her in! She made a *gork* as she **bob**bed on the surface, then **dived** away. Since no **seal**s had eaten the first penguin yet, the others **plop**ped in after her.

"They seem to be making themselves right at home, don't they?" Dr. Drake said, laughing.

"All except our two little **leftover**s from the Penguin **Pavilion**," Nina said.

Only Ernest and Mae remained on land.

They looked up at the Popper children.

They looked down at the cold sea.

Ernest headed into the galley[7] and started making his little-chick *oork* sounds as he **perus**ed the cans of fish.

"I see what you mean," Dr. Drake said, **tap**ping her gloved finger against her lips as she considered the two odd young penguins. "They don't seem to have made any progress getting used to being with other penguins. None at all."

Mae waddled over to the ship's radio and pecked the power button. She lay back and listened to the music, **bouncing** her flippers in rhythm with the **beat**s.

---

7 galley 갤리. 선박이나 항공기 안에 있는 조리실.

HOMECOMING

ONCE THEY HAD finished filling their **bellies** with fish—"And squid," Dr. Drake said, "that's really their primary **diet** around here"—the penguins **filed** onto land. The Poppers and Dr. Drake lined up at the shore to watch. "This is a **novel** environment for the Popper Penguins," Dr. Drake explained while Joel took notes. "They're **bound** to be **apprehensive** about what they'll find. We should expect them to be in**secure** and to stick near the boat for a long time."

As they **emerged** from the surf, though, the Popper Penguins walked in the opposite direction, heading right into the wilds of **Antarctica**. "Oh!" said Dr. Drake.

Once the adult birds had **marche**d past, Mae and Ernest made their sleepy sounds and **toddled** toward their **nest**s in the boat. "Nope," Nina said. "You're not going to bed now—we just got here!"

She and Joel **scoop**ed up the young birds and headed after the line of penguins. Mrs. Popper and Dr. Drake and Yuka **hustled** to **keep up**. "This is most unexpected," Dr. Drake said. "These particular birds have never been to Antarctica, though their **forebear**s of course came from here. Nonetheless, they're taking their **ancestral** routes over the ice. It's as if no time has gone by!"

"Penguins are very smart," Nina said, **nod**ding. "You should have seen Mae at school. Can't say she was much help on my spelling test, though."

"The Popper Penguins seem to be an especially **intelligent line**," Mrs. Popper added. "They were able to learn **sophisticated** dance moves, and their act toured theaters across the country."

"Is it possible that the Popper Penguins have somehow passed along knowledge of where they came from, over all these years?" Yuka asked, **rummaging** through his backpack with his gloved hands to get his research notebook out.

Dr. Drake shook her head. "**Preposterous**. That would require them to have language. Not just simple communication, but the ability to capture verb **tenses**, to **refer** to places by name. Even the most advanced chimpanzees[1] can't do that."

"I think there are a lot of things we might not know about penguins," Nina said, **pat**ting Mae on the head. "I'm positive that she and Ernest have really in-depth conversations with each other."

"Mostly about where their next can of tuna fish is coming from," Joel added.

"I know that to a child's eyes it can seem like animals have magical powers of communication, but the science doesn't **back** that **up**," Dr. Drake said as they marched.

Nina had been working her way ahead of the group. She **whirl**ed around, arms **outstretch**ed. "Then what do you say to *that*?" she asked.

They'd reached a rise in the icy field that looked out over a broad blue-white **valley**. It was covered in hundreds and hundreds of penguins, **waddling to and fro**. They **cluster**ed in the center of the **basin**, where the **dense** crowd

---

1   chimpanzee 침팬지. 포유강 사람과의 하나. 몸의 길이는 63~90센티미터이며, 털은 검은 갈색에 얼굴은 연한 갈색 또는 검은색이다. 어른 개체 중에서는 대머리인 것이 많고 귀가 큰 것이 특징이다. 지능이 발달하였고 무리를 지어 살며 아프리카 대륙에 분포한다.

*ork*ed and *jook*ed and *gaw*ed, **court**ed and **canoodl**ed and fought. Some of the penguins were sitting on nests they'd **cobbl**ed together with small rocks, and before Nina's eyes one toddled over to the nest next door, stole a rock, and waddled it back to his own nest. Then the original owner of the rock **notice**d the theft and waddled over to steal the rock right back, starting a penguin fight that soon **involve**d a half **dozen** neighbors.

Similar episodes were going on throughout the **massive** penguin **colony**. There was so much to see, like in a picture book where each time you looked there was some new tiny story to discover in the **illustration**s.

"This is the biggest gentoo[2] colony in Antarctica," Dr. Drake said proudly. "We've had a continuous study site here for over a hundred years."

"Gentoo?" Joel asked. "What's that?"

"There are many **species** of penguins in the world. Gentoo is the name of the species of the Popper Penguins. My grandfather sent Mr. Popper his original penguin from this very colony."

"Oh," Joel said.

"Oh my!" Mrs. Popper **interrupt**ed. "Have you seen

---

2 gentoo 젠투펭귄. 주로 포클랜드제도나 남극반도 등에 서식하는 펭귄. 현존하는 펭귄 가운데 세 번째로 몸집이 크고 펭귄 중에서 가장 긴 꼬리를 가졌다. 배는 흰색이지만 등과 머리 는 검은색이며, 띠처럼 양쪽 눈 위와 머리 위를 가로지르는 넓은 흰색 무늬가 특징이다.

what's going on over there?"

"That's what I was talking about before!" Nina **protested**. "*Now* do you believe me?"

"Wow," Yuka said.

"Well, I never," Mrs. Popper said.

The Popper Penguins, fresh off their trip from the **Arctic**, had waddled and tobogganed right into the middle of the gentoo colony. There they'd lined up in a row, making quiet *orks* that sounded almost like coughs, waiting for the attention of the other birds. And attention is just what they got. A **ruckus** rose from the colony as they noticed the strangers. Those that weren't **tend**ing nests came right over, crowding in, **knock**ing one another over to get the best view, making a **deafen**ing **chorus** of penguin calls.

Once they had the attention of the other penguins, the Popper Penguins began to perform.

While the Antarctic penguins watched, Patch lay on the ice for a long **pause**, then pretended to wake up and stand and look about. Another penguin joined her, **peering** about **dramatic**ally. They were followed by ten more, until there were twelve penguins in all. They marched in a perfect circle, all waddling in **unison**, then formed a square before becoming a semicircle. Two of them **separate**d from the group and got into a **mock** fight, **buffeting** each other with their flippers and **biting** the air. They both fell over, as

140

if dead.

"They're performing Nelson and Columbus!" Nina **exclaim**ed.

"Oh no, does that mean the **ladder**-and-board act from the original show is next?" Joel asked, covering his eyes. "I heard that was a complete **disaster**."

As they watched, the twelve penguins marched in **formation** up an ice **cliff**, where they crowded at the **summit**. Then they went completely still.

"What's supposed to happen now?" Mrs. Popper asked.

"I'm not sure," Joel said.

The audience of a thousand penguins and five humans

began to **murmur.**

Then Patch **let out** an ear-**piercing** cry. As one, the penguins made a great show of pushing one another to the ground, tobogganing off the **peak** in all directions, letting out loud **squawks** as they **tumbled** away before getting to their feet again down at the bottom, appearing very proud of themselves. It all looked a bit like a firework **display,** only made of penguins.

Once they were finished, the Popper Penguins lined themselves back up in a straight line, while the Antarctic penguins **broke out** into a **raucous** chorus of *orks* and *gaws*. The Popper Penguins took **neat bows,** or at least as best they were able with their **stout** bodies. (It was difficult to bow without a waist.)

The gentoos **surged** forward, crowding around the Popper Penguins, **greeting** them with a **frantic** display of **clacking beaks** and loud calls. They lifted the Popper Penguins so they surfed over the top of the colony, making *orks* of **delight** as they accepted the crowd's **admiration.**

"Well, I'll be!" Yuka said.

"The scientific world has never seen anything like this," Dr. Drake **marveled.**

"The Popper Penguins **passed down** stories about Antarctica *and* Stillwater!" Nina said.

"Maybe they'll keep passing these stories down in the

wild colony here," Yuka **proposed**.

"**Fascinating**," said Dr. Drake. "We'll need to publish studies on this right away. Are you prepared to work with me, Yuka?"

"I'm **revising** my **dissertation** in my head right now!" he said. He and Dr. Drake then **descend**ed into a lot of scientific language that Nina and Joel couldn't understand at all.

Their attention was soon drawn to the young **chicks** at their feet. Mae and Ernest had enjoyed the Popper show, jumping up and down in **glee** and doing their own pantomime[3] version of the specialized steps along with the Popper Penguins. But now they looked almost **mournful**. Head down, Ernest was already making his slow waddling progress back to the boat. Mae made an *oork* that sounded very familiar to the Popper kids by now: She was ready for some canned tuna fish. Ernest made an *oork* that they also knew very well: It was time for his favorite nature program on the ship's shortwave[4] radio.

Joel gave Nina a long look. Their plan for getting the two young chicks back to the wild wasn't working out. Not at all.

---

3   pantomime 팬터마임. 배우가 대사 없이 표정과 몸짓만으로 내용을 전달하는 연극.
4   shortwave 단파(短波). 파장 10~100미터, 진동수 3~30메가헤르츠(MHz)의 전자파로, 지표면과 지상 100~300킬로미터 높이에 있는 전리층(電離層)의 아래층에서 반사되기 때문에 원거리 무선 전신, 대외 방송 등에 이용된다.

FAREWELL, DR. DRAKE

WHILE JOEL AND Nina **holed up** in the research station,
they heard a **clamor** from the icy **valley** as the Popper
Penguins gave yet another **command** performance.

The Popper children weren't out enjoying the show,
though—they were too worried about Mae and Ernest.
The young penguins were eating dried squid from a **pile**
on the floor, in between moves in their version of chess.
Joel and Nina hadn't been able to **figure out** the rules yet,

but it seemed to **involve** a lot of **peck**ing and fighting and pawns[1] flying everywhere.

"It's almost like they don't know that they're penguins," Joel said.

"I'd say that's exactly right," Dr. Drake said from the **doorway**. Nina and Joel looked up, **startled**. "When they're born, young birds go through a process called **imprint**ing. In order to learn the right habits and bird manners, they study whatever animal they first see when they **hatch**. Normally that's another penguin, of course. In this case, though, it was you!"

"But the original Popper Penguins were able to go live in the wild," Nina **protest**ed.

Dr. Drake **nod**ded. "You'll remember that Mr. Popper's first penguin, Captain Cook, was an adult. When *he* was a **chick**, he'd been around other penguins. By the time chicks were in Stillwater, they had other penguins around to imprint on. These two weren't in the same situation, **unfortunately**. It's not your fault—you did the best you could with these eggs. But I'm afraid they won't survive out here in the wild without parents, just like human children wouldn't."

---

1 pawn 폰. 체스에서 사용하는 말 가운데 하나. 게임을 시작할 때는 1칸 또는 2칸을 갈 수 있으며 이외에는 한 번에 1칸을 전진할 수 있고, 대각선 방향에 있는 상대방 말을 잡을 수 있다.

With that, Mae **let out** a loud squid **burp** as she picked up a black rook[2] with her **beak**, **deft**ly **deposit**ing it on the other side of the board. Ernest **squawk**ed in **outrage** at the move, then **settled down**. He gently **tap**ped each of the white pieces with his beak, considering his options.

"It's true, there aren't many chess sets in the wild," Joel said.

"Or nature hours for Ernest to listen to on the radio," Nina added.

"I **suspect** these aren't gentoos, either, but Magellanic penguins.[3] Those penguins don't even live in the **Antarctic**, but in South America. To be honest, Ernest might be female and Mae might be male. I could be wrong on that, though—even after all these years working with penguins, it's still hard for me to tell the sexes apart without a blood test."

"Oh my," Nina said.

Just then there was a clamor outside as the Popper Penguins finished their big act. Mrs. Popper and Yuka **burst** in, **breathless**. "This was the best show yet!" Mrs. Popper said. "The Popper Penguins have really gotten their

---

2 rook 룩. 체스에서 사용하는 말 가운데 하나. 가로 또는 세로 방향으로 경기자가 원하는 칸만큼 전진 또는 후진할 수 있다.

3 Magellanic penguin 마젤란펭귄. 마젤란해협이나 포클랜드제도 등에 서식하는 펭귄으로 눈썹에서 머리 옆과 목 앞으로 돌아가면서 흰 띠가 있고, 가슴에는 굵고 가는 검은색 띠가 두 줄 있다.

comic timing down. I'm proud of them."

"At least the Popper Penguins have found a good home," Joel said. "They're basically **celebrities** down here."

Nina threw her arms around her mother's waist, **bury**ing her face in the pockets of her **puffy** coat. "Mae and Ernest aren't even the same *species* as all these other penguins, Mom," she cried.

"Oh dear," Mrs. Popper said. "What would you suggest, Dr. Drake? What's best for our little penguins?"

"They can't live in the wild, but they could do a lot of good for the penguins that *do*," Dr. Drake said. "As the planet warms from human activity, this ice is **melt**ing, and the penguins' homeland is in greater and greater danger. Sometimes we lose entire **colonies** of penguins because of the melting ice down here. It sounds like the Penguin **Pavilion** didn't do things right, but *you* could. What if you brought Mae and Ernest to visit schools in the winter, when it's cold enough for them to be **out and about**, so kids everywhere could learn about penguins? Other times of year, scientists and interested children could come visit your birds in your **frozen basement**. I'm sure the Popper **Foundation** would be interested in funding such a place, with you as the **caretaker**."

Mrs. Popper looked surprised. "Money has been tight, and I'd be **honor**ed to do something to help the penguins. I've been making some charcoal[4] sketches of the Popper show. Maybe I could sell art of Mae and Ernest, to support the Popper Foundation's work."

Nina kept her arms around her mother but pulled her head back to look up, **amazed**. "Really?" she said, her face **streak**ed with tears.

Joel jumped up and down. "This is amazing! We're going to keep Mae and Ernest!"

The penguins in question **scold**ed the humans for their **interrupt**ion, before returning to their chess game.

"I'm going to stay down here with Dr. Drake, writing my **dissertation** on the **transmission** of knowledge between **generation**s of gentoo penguins," Yuka said. "But I'll need to go back up to Stillwater first to **draft** my study plan with my professor. I could take you—and our two young penguin **ambassador**s—up with me."

"That's great news, Yuka," Mrs. Popper said. "And great news for the gentoo penguins, that they'll be the subjects of your study."

"It's just about as far away from home as an Inuit can get," he said. "My family will miss me for a few years."

"I'm sure they'll be very proud of your **contribution** to science," Mrs. Popper said.

---

4 charcoal 목탄. 버드나무나 오동나무 등을 구워서 만든 가느다란 막대 모양의 소묘 재료. 연필과 달리 연하고 입자가 거친 것이 특징이다.

148

"I hope so!"

And so it was that only a few days later, the Popper family and their two young penguins lined up at the **stern** of the boat. "Just think, Joel!" Nina said. "We're going to be bringing our penguins back to school, after all!"

"And for a good purpose this time," Joel added.

The boat began to pull away from the **dock**. In **unison**, Mae and Ernest made a new kind of noise, a sort of *yewk*.

"What does that call mean?" Mrs. Popper asked as she waved goodbye to Dr. Drake.

"I think it means they're **content**," Joel said.

"'Content,'" Nina said. "That word was on my spelling test, once upon a time."

"Content is a very nice thing for a young penguin to be," Mrs. Popper said.

Yuka **blast**ed the boat's horn, and with that sound the Poppers waved goodbye to **Antarctica**. Joel and Nina lifted the penguins so that they could say goodbye, too, which they did **dramatic**ally, waving their **flipper**s as hard as they could. Then Yuka sped the boat up, and they were **plow**ing through the waves, heading back home and to whatever adventures it held **in store**.

ork!